LUTON SIXTH FORM COLLEGE

Macmillan Modern Dramatists
Series Editors: Bruce and Adele King

**Published titles**

Reed Anderson, *Federico Garcia Lorca*
Eugene Benson, *J. M. Synge*
Renate Benson, *German Expressionist Drama*
Normand Berlin, *Eugene O'Neill*
Michael Billington, *Alan Ayckbourn*
Roger Boxill, *Tennessee Williams*
John Bull, *New British Political Dramatists*
Dennis Carroll, *David Mamet*
Neil Carson, *Arthur Miller*
Maurice Charney, *Joe Orton*
Ruby Cohn, *New American Dramatists, 1960–1980*
Bernard F. Dukore, *American Dramatists, 1918–1945*
Bernard F. Dukore, *Harold Pinter*
Michael Etherton, *Contemporary Irish Dramatists*
Arthur Ganz, *George Bernard Shaw*
James Gibbs, *Wole Soyinka*
Frances Gray, *John Arden*
Frances Gray, *Noel Coward*
Charles Hayter, *Gilbert and Sullivan*
Julian Hilton, *Georg Büchner*
David Hirst, *Edward Bond*
David Hirst, *Dario Fo and Franca Rame*
Helene Keyssar, *Feminist Theatre*
Bettina L. Knapp, *French Theatre 1918–1939*
Tom Leabhart, *Mime and Post-Modern Mime*
Glenon Leeming, *Poetic Drama*
Charles Lyons, *Samuel Beckett*
Gerry McCarthy, *Edward Albee*
Jan McDonald, *The New Drama 1900–1914*
Susan Bassnett-McGuire, *Luigi Pirandello*
Margery Morgan, *August Strindberg*
Leonard C. Pronko, *Eugene Labiche and Georges Feydean*
Jeanette L. Savona, *Jean Genet*
Claude Schumacher, *Alfred Jarry and Guillaume Apollinaire*
Laurence Senelick, *Anton Chekhov*
Theodore Shank, *American Alternative Theatre*
James Simmons, *Sean O'Casey*
Ronald Speirs, *Bertolt Brecht*
David Thomas, *Henrik Ibsen*
Dennis Walder, *Athol Fugard*
Thomas Whitaker, *Tom Stoppard*
Nick Worrall, *Nikolai Gogol and Ivan Turgenev*
Katharine Worth, *Oscar Wilde*

**Further titles in preparation**

MACMILLAN MODERN DRAMATISTS

# DARIO FO
# and
# FRANCA RAME

## David Hirst

Lecturer in Drama
University of Birmingham

**MACMILLAN**

© David Hirst 1989

First published 1989

Published by
Higher and Further Education Division
MACMILLAN PUBLISHERS LTD
Houndmills, Basingstoke, Hampshire RG21 2XS
and London
Companies and representatives
throughout the world

Typeset by Wessex Typesetters
(Division of The Eastern Press Ltd)
Frome, Somerset

Printed in China

British Library Cataloguing in Publication Data
Hirst, David L. (David Lawrence), 1942–
Dario Fo and Franca Rame.
1. Drama in Italian. Fo, Dario, 1926– &
Rame, Franca
I. Title
852'.914'09
ISBN 0–333–39601–4
ISBN 0–333–39602–2 Pbk

Per Bruno,
mio secondo padre

# Contents

# List of Plates

1. Fo in his most celebrated piece: *Mistero buffo*.
2–7: The Fo–Rame partnership in a wide variety of plays:
2. *Settimo: ruba un po' meno (Seventh Commandment: Steal A Bit Less)*, 1964.
3. *La signora è da buttare (The Woman Should Be Kicked Out)*, R.A.I. television, 1977.
4. Rehearsing *Tutta casa, letto e chiesa (Female Parts)* in 1978.
5. *Arlecchino*, 1985.
6. *Clacson, trombette e pernacchi (Trumpets and Raspberries)*, 1981.
7. *Quasi per caso una donna: Elisabetta (Elizabeth, Almost By Accident A Woman)*, 1984.
8. Rame's great breakthrough role: the Mother of Michele Lu Lanzone in *L'Operaio conosce 300 parole (The Worker Knows 300 Words)*, 1969.
9. Rame in *Una donna sola (A Woman Alone)* from *Female Parts*, 1977.
10. Rame in *Arlecchino*, 1985.
11. Fo as Giovanni in *Non si paga, non si paga! (Can't Pay? Won't Pay!)*. Revival (revised version), 1980.
12. Fo as Arlecchino, 1985.

# Acknowledgements

My thanks are due to Dario Fo and Franca Rame, for their generosity and assistance; Laura Lombardi of the Piccolo Teatro, who furnished me with much valuable material; Marco Fiocchi, for his help and advice; Arturo Vita, for his hospitality; and Gianfranco Barbieri, whose lectures on social and political issues in modern Italy proved inspirational.

D. H.

# Editors' Preface

The *Macmillan Modern Dramatists* is an international series of introductions to major and significant nineteenth- and twentieth-century dramatists, movements and new forms of drama in Europe, Great Britain, America and new nations such as Nigeria and Trinidad. Besides new studies of great and influential dramatists of the past, the series includes volumes on contemporary authors, recent trends in the theatre and on many dramatists, such as writers of farce, who have created theatre 'classics' while being neglected by literary criticism. The volumes in the series devoted to individual dramatists include a biography, a survey of the plays, and detailed analysis of the most significant plays, along with discussion, where relevant, of the political, social, historical and theatrical context. The authors of the volumes, who are involved with theatre as playwrights, directors, actors, teachers and critics, are concerned with the plays as theatre and discuss such matters as performance, character interpretation and staging, along with themes and context.

BRUCE KING
ADELE KING

# 1
# Italy and Britain

Credo che il successo che hanno i nostri testi in tutta
l'Europa e in tutto il mondo è determinato dal fatto che
noi proponiamo dei problemi che tutta la gente ha
bisogno di sentir dibattuti, sia in Germania che in
Francia o in Svezia. A me non importa niente che mi si
venga a dire che esiste il teatro italiano. Che cosè il
teatro italiano? Quale teatro italiano? Mi sento molto
più europeo.

[I'm convinced that the success of our plays throughout
Europe and the rest of the world is attributable to the
fact that we raise issues which everybody needs to
hear discussed, whether it be in Germany, France or
Switzerland. I couldn't care less when people come up
to me and say thanks to me Italian theatre exists. What
is Italian theatre? Which Italian theatre? Rather I feel
myself to be European.]

(Dario Fo, *La sinistra,* 29 May 1979)

My introduction to the work of Dario Fo was in July 1979 when I went to a performance of *Accidental Death of an Anarchist* at the Half Moon Theatre. The performance was unique for two reasons: it was the day Margaret Thatcher began her first term as Prime Minister (a defeat for socialism which shattered the British Left), and it was the occasion of a special gala to raise funds for the family of Blair Peach, the man (accidentally) killed by the police during a race riot in London's East End. Commenting on the Conservative electoral victory, Andrew de la Tour, the actor playing the Superintendent in the production, announced after the show, 'There are dark days in store for us now': the events of the play – the accidental killing of the anarchist, the police cover-up, the amassing of the forces of reaction and oppression – seemed all too relevant in modern Britain. Though nothing of the drama's exuberant farce was missing, the comedy seemed actually to underline, to bring out, the serious issues at stake.

In 1981, following the success of *Anarchist*, Rob Walker's production of *Can't Pay? Won't Pay!* – the play which in a fringe production had served to launch Fo in Britain in 1978 – was revived in the West End. By contrast this show seemed superficial, slight, bearing little relevance to contemporary Britain and losing in a plethora of cheap gags and self-indulgent actors' mannerisms the serious social or political elements of the drama. I found it very hard to recognise in this production the play I had seen performed in Milan by Dario Fo, Franca Rame and their company the previous year. For one thing the London show ran for two hours; the Milanese one started at 9 p.m. and the theatre was still buzzing with life when I had to leave well after midnight. I was aware that Fo had revised the play (originally performed in 1974), adding a series of new issues: discussion of the recent sacking of thousands of Fiat workers and a critique of Pope Wojtyla (John Paul II), for instance, with a comparison between the situation in Turin and that in Gdansk. I relished too Fo's enjoyment of improvisation, as in his elaborate criticism (through his character, Giovanni) of selfish drivers – a comic *tour de force* cut short at the performance I saw by Franca Rame silencing him with a shout of 'Dario, basta!' ('Dario, enough!').

And I was intrigued by the members of the audience, whose participation in the open discussion which followed the show served to protract the performance well into the night. I found it difficult to equate the mixture of comedy and seriousness, the skilful return to the central political issues despite the apparently inexhaustible series of comic inventions, with the triviality, irrelevance and flimsiness of the British production.

Gradually, through a detailed study of the originals and their adaptations, I have come to realise the extent to which the dramas performed under Fo's name in Britain differ from his own vital brand of theatre. The *Anarchist* production – coinciding as it did with a particular climate in British political life which was uncomfortably close to the events in Italy that had inspired Fo's play – was unique. As Gavin Richards, who played the Maniac, has said, the play was 'smacking home suddenly'. Moreover, within two weeks the company had raised a thousand pounds for the Blair Peach Fund. This may seem small beer compared with the hundreds of thousands Fo and Rame have collected over the years for various political causes: from the Palestine Liberation Organisation to Soccorso Rosso, the organisation run by Franca Rame which was born of the company's work in Milan and which devotes its energies to helping political prisoners. The original British production of *Anarchist* cannot be faulted in its aim and intention: to perform relevant, vital and popular political theatre in venues off the mainstream West End theatre circuit. The company faced a fascinating crisis of conscience when, after their triumphant success at the Half Moon, they were invited by Donald Albery to transfer the show to the West End. When they did so, the production changed radically: the script was not altered, but the fact of playing in front of another audience with different political commitments and over a long period of time meant that inevitably the crucial relationship between serious satire and broad comedy was gradually eroded and eventually lost altogether. The irony in this is twofold. In the first place the West End success of *Anarchist*, followed by the even longer run of *Can't Pay? Won't Pay!*, set a style for the playing of Fo's work and an attitude to his drama on the part of performers, managers and audiences (to say nothing of critics) which is at the furthest extreme from the way his plays are performed and received in Italy. He has always worked within a company which – despite the radical changes in theatrical organisation which resulted from the decision of Fo and Rame to quit the bourgeois theatre circuit in 1968 – he has effectively managed. He writes his own plays, acts in them and both directs and designs them. He has, since the late 1950s, enjoyed an unprecedented popular success which accounts for his skill in winning new audiences amongst the workers and students after the turbulent challenges of the political crisis in the late 1960s. The audiences to which he has played and the venues in which he has performed are at the furthest remove from those which characterise either the commercial British theatre or the fringe.

Yet the success of the two farces opened up an interest in this dramatist, who has been one of the most vital forces in Italian theatre for thirty years and whose work was well known on the continent long before it enjoyed performance in Britain. Following *Can't Pay? Won't Pay!* and *Anarchist*, the National Theatre mounted a production of *Female Parts* (1981), a series of monologues which were largely the inspiration of Franca Rame. In 1985 a third farce was performed in the West End: *Trumpets and Raspberries*. All four of these pieces have been performed in the United States (the last under the far cleverer title, *About Face*), and they have become well-tried standbys elsewhere: repertory companies in Britain constantly produce the three farces, whilst *Female Parts*, in its entirety or (more often) in an abbreviated version, has become a standard item in the fringe actress's repertoire. Fo himself, when he did his workshops at the Riverside Studios, London, in April and May 1983 – an event which had a profound influence on the British fringe, inspiring a host of productions and even the formation of one company, the Fo–Rame Theatre Group – commented in characteristically pragmatic vein on the nature and effect of the *Anarchist* West End transfer:

The danger of being instrumentalised by economic power is always there. However, what you have to consider is how much of your politics you are able to continue to get through, even when performing in a commercial situation. For example, *Accidental Death* ran for almost a year in East London, performed by the same company. At a certain point the director of the theatre to which they transferred in the West End came and invited them to perform in the West End. The actors in the company went through a crisis because they didn't know whether to accept or not. Later though, I talked with a lot of English comrades who saw the show in the West End, and they said that this transfer was a correct political decision. Because, if nothing else, it enabled people to see a style, theatrical language and technique, which otherwise they might never have seen. And not only the technique but also the content, the politics of it. And perhaps if that show had never gone into the West End, then I would never have had the chance to come to London myself.

*(Red Notes*, 1983, p. 43)

His plays, it is true, are being seen in Britain but acted in a style quite alien at times to Fo's intention and in adaptations which – certainly in the case of all three farces – are so far from the originals as to be theatrical works in their own right. Moreover, by the time *Anarchist* reached the West End it had lost some of its bite. Divorced from the more immediate issues of Blair Peach's murder and the change of government, the force and relevance of the satire was diminished. Fo's play uses the anarchist's death as the starting-point for an examination of the wholesale manipulation of information following the Piazza Fontana bombing in Milan in 1969, which was blamed on left-wing terrorists. He wrote this work in response to demands from his audience to dramatise the real facts in the 'strategy of tension' which continued and developed as a major politicial and social reality in Italy all through the 1970s. For this reason he constantly updated and revised the play, one of the few works which he kept consistently in the repertoire for several years. But, by the time an effective end to terrorism had been brought about through the methods of General Alberto dalla Chiesa and the fascist group responsible for the bomb had been brought to justice a decade after the event, Fo's play had served its purpose. By this time he was absorbed in very different issues.

Fo writes for the moment. His drama is inspired by contemporary Italian affairs. As he said – with a true relish of paradox – on the BBC *Arena* television programme dedicated to his work,

> Seriously, I want to be a classic, and just like the classic writers, I try to do things that are ephemeral. The Greeks used to write tragedies to be performed only a few times. They were produced to be destroyed . . . and burned the day they were performed. Shakespeare didn't write for posterity, no way . . . .

The performance of his plays outside Italy – and particularly the revival of earlier work abroad – therefore presents a particular problem. This is compounded by the fact of the long runs his plays have enjoyed in Britain. Fo rarely revises one of his old works in the theatre. The revival of *Can't Pay? Won't Pay!* in 1980 was an exception, and then it was considerably rewritten. The only piece he has continued to perform over a long period is *Mistero buffo* (*Comic Mystery*, 1969) – his irreverent re-creation of medieval stories – which is also the work he has most consistently elaborated and revised, altering not only the individual stories themselves, but also the interludes or digressions between them, such as the ever-expanding satire of Pope Wojtyła , whose attitude Fo now cunningly pretends to confuse with that of his monstrous creation Pope Bonifacio VIII.

Fo does not so much revive his plays as *rework* them. For example, *Ordine, per Dio.OOO.OOO.OOO!* (*Order, for Goooooooooood!*, 1972) is an extended two-act version of an earlier piece: *Il telaio* (*The Loom*), 1969), a play about the exploitation of piece-work labourers. Again, *Parliamo di donne* (*Let's Talk about Women*, 1977) is an anthology of several extracts from earlier plays performed by Franca Rame. More intriguingly, Fo reworks theatrical ideas and devices. Thus in an early play, *Aveva due pistole con gli occhi bianchi e neri* (*He Had Two Pistols with Black and White Eyes*, 1960) – a good example of his taste for bizarre titles – he exploits the farcical idea of a double: the lead actor (Fo) plays the contrasting roles of a priest who has lost his memory and a leader of the Milanese underworld. In a much later play, *Clacson, trombette e pernacchie* (*Horns, Hooters and Raspberries* [*Trumpets and Raspberries*], 1981), the device reappears as he doubles the roles of a Fiat worker and the head of the company, Gianni Agnelli, who as a result of facial surgery following a car accident is made to resemble his employee exactly. Since Agnelli has supposedly been kidnapped, *Clacson* was in turn a reworking of ideas in *Il Fanfani rapito* (*Fanfani Kidnapped*, 1975), in which another leading Italian figure – Amintore Fanfani, the secretary of the Christian Democrat Party – is the victim of a plot engineered by his fellow politician Andreotti to ensure that he will not be an embarrassment to the party in the forthcoming elections. Fo was able to make fun of Fanfani's notoriously small stature by employing an old theatrical trick he had used previously in *La colpa è sempre del diavolo* (*It's Always the Devil's Fault*, 1965). When, two years later – in 1977 – he revived *La signora è da buttare* (*The Woman Should be Kicked Out*) for an RAI television presentation, he completely rewrote the work, introducing a dwarf St George (whose legs had been reduced to stumps through a fall from heaven) attacking a nine-foot-high dragon symbolising ecology.

Whilst giving us some idea of the ingenuity of Fo as a theatrical artist, these examples also emphasise the fact that it is particularly important in discussing his theatre to have a clear idea of what constitutes the text. We must certainly remove from our consideration all literary definitions, as Fo has made clear in refuting the idea that he is a poet:

> I've always thought of poets as people in a higher sphere, those creatures with laurel and myrtle leaves on their forehead, and tied to considerations of the world which are not quite 'civil' in the Latin sense of the word: which is used to describe a person who takes part in everyday life and is directly involved with social and political issues, finding these inseparable from his relationship with other people. The poet is someone who cuts himself off from any actual problem, from reality and from the mundane. He is someone who doesn't ever risk getting his hands really dirty. Dante, for instance, isn't worthy of his bust; for me the real poets are Petrarch, Cavalcanti, Villon . . . What am I? I'm a theatrical practitioner, an artisan.
>
> (*Moda*, 2 Nov. 1985)

Or consider Franca Rame's description of his work:

> At this point I should say something about Dario's craft as a writer, or I should say, as a maker of scripts for the stage. Why a maker rather than writer? Because, when he writes, Dario needs to think out and build a stage or, preferably, a sequence of scenic spaces and planes on which the dramatic action can take place. It is also a question of theatrical construction rather than simple writing because his theatre is not based on characters, but on situations. The characters become masks, i.e. emblematic pretexts at the service of a situation. The stage moves on by virtue of an action,

just as the actor moves by virtue of his gestures and his words. Even the stage props therefore become part of an action. This demands great open-mindedness at the level of stage management. Therefore Dario can allow himself to bring on to the stage puppets and marionettes, masks and mannikins, actors with natural or painted faces. And all this he joins together from the inside with the songs, the jokes, the coarse shouting, the use of noisy instruments, the pauses, the exasperated rhythm – though never overdone, because his style is rigorous even when everything seems haphazard and accidental. Only superficial people can in fact think that Dario's theatre is 'handmade'. On the contrary, it is all reasoned out in advance, written, rehearsed, rewritten and rehearsed again and always in a practical relationship to and with the audience.

(Introduction to *Can't Pay? Won't Pay!*, 1982, pp. xi–xii)

'A theatrical text', according to Fo, 'is really a musical score, with its rhythms, its silences and its pauses.' One gains little from reading a score; it needs to be performed. If the same is true of a play, it is even more true of the non-literary drama produced by Fo.

Fo's plays are written very quickly. Franca Rame states that it took him twenty days to write *Gli archangeli non giocono a flipper* (*The Archangels Don't Play Pinball*, 1959), which represents a record: normally he works much more speedily. In the case of *Pum, pum. Chi è? La polizia!* (*Knock, Knock. Who's There? The Police!*, 1972) he had finished the first act in two days. He gave it to the company to read through, and, having gained their approval, locked himself in a hotel room for another two days and finished the play. Of course, the ideas, having been researched over a much longer period of time, had been maturing for months, even years.

The text is not fixed once the play goes into rehearsal. Quite the reverse: it is subjected to constant changes before being presented to an audience. Fo still encourages a series of previews where the audience is asked to comment on the play and offer suggestions as to how it may be improved. He is proud of the fact that the resultant drama is a genuinely communal affair:

> With *Can't Pay? Won't Pay!* above all we pursued the technique of 'verifying the text' with an audience of workers, the people who lived in the area in which we were performing. We played it in front of them and as a result it was necessary to 'correct' certain characters following on from the observations they made, as well as to *rewrite the ending* completely. From the very beginning this is what we have always done with our brand of political theatre.
>
> (C. Valentini, *La storia di Dario Fo*, 1977, p. 159)

Moreover – and *Can't Pay? Won't Pay!* is a particularly good example – the performance text is a *scenario* rather than a set script. It is deliberately conceived in such a way as to allow for improvisation and adaptation according to the particular circumstances and conditions of performance.

Nor is this the end of the complex theatrical process which characterises the relationship between Fo and his audience. When they first broke with the commercial theatre circuit in 1968 and began to perform through Communist Party venues, Fo's company invented what became known as the 'third act' of their drama. This was the discussion which followed the show, often as long and as turbulent as the performance itself. There exist three types of printed text of Fo's work: the standard Einaudi collected edition (now in its sixth volume); the texts – with documentation and illustrations – published by Fo's theatrical organisation, La Comune; and two volumes of collected plays published by Mazzotta and entitled *Compagni senza censura* (*Uncensored Comrades*). The last of these represents an attempt to assemble the full 'text' of the earlier political dramas (those composed from 1969 to 1972) by printing along with the acting script the *interventi*: the audience discussion which followed. By comparing the three types of published edition it becomes clear that, in the context of Fo's theatre, the term 'text' extends to every element that constitutes performance: all the various details which characterise the process of the drama's creation and its communication.

It is worth glancing at one or two of these audience *interventi*, since they tell us a great deal about the playgoers and about their different responses to and effect on Fo's work. His drama *L'operaio conosce trecento parole, il padrone mille; per questo lui è il padrone* (*The Worker Knows 300 Words, the Boss 1000; That's Why he's the Boss*, 1969) was performed – and deliberately set – in a *casa del popolo*, a workers' club, and made a critical examination of the history of communism. Here are two responses: from (1) a worker and (2) a militant member of the Communist Party.

[1] Everyone was looking for a worker, well I'm a worker, from the Trullo zone, because it seemed to me that if there wasn't a worker who would join in the debate, people wouldn't be satisfied. I believe the worker and the intellectual must work together, as I consider the intellectual who comes into my factory a

12

member of the proletariat because he's fighting the struggle with me. I want to make one thing clear; I live in the suburbs, not in a prefab but in council accommodation [*casa popolare*]; however, the conditions are much the same: there's no road, no sewer, and if the priest who spoke earlier wants to call me 'poor', let him, but I'm a worker, I've understood what class struggle is, and I'm a Communist, not a pauper. I'd like, though, to give an invitation to the ARCI [the Communist organisation through which Fo at this point was working] and the Nuova Scena Company: you need to go where the workers really are; there aren't many here, you need to drop into the suburbs, the poor areas. It's true that the company has a lot on its plate, but it's true as well that the students and university comrades could organise certain types of show – like this one, or different – and discuss with workers in their area. Mind you, really dealing with the problems of that particular area, so as to get into the workers' head some things that would give them a broader view of the political battle that needs fighting.

(*Compagni senza censura*, vol. 1, 1970, p. 180)

[2] I want to start with the words of Mayakovsky: you said that if the weak unite, walk shoulder to shoulder, it will be difficult for anyone to defeat them; capitalism still lives, etc. You tonight don't strike me as having walked shoulder to shoulder very much with the workers' movement and with the Communist Party in particular. You've just revealed all the negative sides of the party, no positive side has been pointed out or brought forward. You've tried to save tonight's performance by quoting the words of Mayakovsky that we know and appreciate. However, given that you

consider yourselves a class theatre it doesn't seem to me you've done much to promote a positive struggle within the workers' movement. The role you've played in the class struggle represents a moment of recession; some of the comments you've made tonight you ought to leave to the fascists. (Ibid., p. 185)

A very different response greeted *Anarchist*; this drama was provocative in a different way. Unlike *L'operaio*, which was written with the express aim of provoking (positive) analysis within the party – and which it failed to do, leading instead to a rift between Fo and the Italian Communist Party (PCI) – *Anarchist*, written immediately after Fo had quit the Communist circuit, was designed instead to stir up a sense of outrage. This comment by an Italcantieri worker is typical of the reactions aroused:

Brother workers. I want to say something too. The show that Dario Fo's company have performed is something really important in every way. It shoes how the bourgeois State restrains and kills all the time the class that fights it, that is the working class. The other day at Italcantieri a worker of fifty-six died. The bourgeois newspapers say it was a heart attack, so it's something accidental, just like what happened to Pinelli. But this worker died as a result of exploitation, doing piece work, really working just like an animal. Today, so that we can have unity within the working class, we need to speak out clearly.

(*Compagni senza censura*, vol. 2, p. 217)

These comments – sometimes deeply critical, sometimes more a statement of personal feeling than a direct response to the issues dramatised – nevertheless testify to the vitality and immediacy of Fo's theatre. Moreover, when we realise, as Franca Rame has pointed out, that in their first year working the ARCI circuit the company played to 200,000 people 70 per cent of whom had never been in a theatre before, and that when they broke with this to operate their own collective, La Comune, they immediately acquired 6000 subscriptions, which within a month had grown to 18,000, it is abundantly clear that we are dealing with a theatrical phenomenon which has no parallel in Britain or America.

Fo combines the appeal of a celebrated comic performer with the talents of a director committed to popular political theatre. It was particularly fascinating, therefore, to observe a programme organised by British commercial television in December 1985 which brought together two very different people, Griff Rhys Jones and John McGrath, to watch and discuss various video extracts of Fo at work. Griff Rhys Jones is one of Britain's most successful television comics, and it was for him that the production of *Trumpets and Raspberries* was mounted; McGrath has distinguished himself as a theatrical practitioner who, after following a university career, has devoted himself – notably through his shows for 7:84 Scotland – to rediscovering popular working class theatre with a political basis. Watching and listening to these two theatrical practitioners – representative of the two sides of Fo's creativity – was salutary. The strengths of his theatre emerged the more clearly, whilst the (almost wilful) misinterpretation of his work in Britain coupled with the inability of the British theatre to forge a genuinely productive alliance between popular dramatic forms and political education was underlined.

Griff Rhys Jones – wonderful entertainer though he is, and inventive though his performance of the twin figures in *Trumpets and Raspberries* was – is perfectly illustrative of the performer who lacks the feature which Fo considers most important to his theatre: an ideological commitment. Fo chose to open his discussion at the Riverside Studios in 1973 by asserting,

> I think that in order to open a discussion, a dialogue, it would be good if I were to say a few things which I consider fundamental in theatre work.
>
> It is essential that this work, work in the theatre, has an ideological moment behind it. What do I mean by ideological? To have an understanding of why people move in particular ways, what lies behind their style of gesture, the way they use their voices, etc. also why one would choose one particular text to perform rather than another. And why one would choose to perform a given piece in an epic style rather than naturalistically.
>
> (*Red Notes*, 1983, p. 1)

The simple reason why *Trumpets and Raspberries* was chosen for performance in Britain was that it was seen to provide a vehicle for Griff Rhys Jones. The original motivation which lay behind the choice of *Can't Pay? Won't Pay!* and *Anarchist* by Belt and Braces was entirely lacking. The reasons for the revival of these shows by repertory companies throughout Britain, however, smack all too often of opportunism coupled with an element of hypocrisy: ostensibly radical political theatre is being offered, when in fact it is the cosier appeal of the comedy which is the real attraction. Fo has in this way become a respectable writer in the trendy bourgeois theatre: a fate which he deplores and which he does not deserve. The problem in Britain is the lack of collective thinking and political motivation within the theatre. Whilst the designer and the director of *Trumpets and Raspberries* both hold pronouncedly Marxist views, these were subverted by the style and intention of the show. The opposite approach does, it must be admitted, lead to a criticism often voiced in Italy: that, apart from the two leading performers, Fo's company is composed of actors chosen more for their ideological solidarity than for their histrionic skills. But that is an exaggeration.

Certainly Fo never falls into the traps which beset the British Left. McGrath, though undoubtedly sincere in his concern to bring popular theatre to workers in Scotland, simply does not have vital traditions of drama on which to draw. He himself admits that Fo goes back to the Middle Ages in the forms he employs, whilst the British artist is obliged to draw on the more recent traditions of pantomime and music hall (which have long since lost much of their popular appeal). There is a tendency on the part of British political dramatists to overestimate the significance and force of outmoded theatrical genres which they feel it is their duty to employ in addressing themselves directly to a working-class audience. It is a tendency observable also in the work of John Arden and Margaretta D'Arcy in Ireland. When we consider the variety and breadth of Fo's work, the scope of their achievement appears very limited, whilst their attitude courts a danger Fo has always assiduously avoided and which he describes in a reference to Brecht: 'The people can say deep and complex things with great simplicity. The popularists who descend from above to write for the people repeat hollow banalties with great complexity,' (Introduction to *Can't Pay? Won't Pay!*, 1982, p. x).

Significantly, McGrath is critical of what he calls Fo's anti-intellectualism. But when he makes heavy weather of the Fo sketch about St Benedict by referring to the

Maoist concept of Lao Dung and insists that the monoloque describing Zanni's hunger from *Mistero Buffo* is concerned with an 'infantile psychological moment' which 'underpins his more articulate critique of consumerist society' (this is a piece about starvation!) we observe an altogether different type of theatrical mind at work. It is one which finds Fo's style ultimately 'oppressive', which claims his drama is 'non-political because not class political', and which demands to know what St Benedict has to do with the Cultural Revolution.

To answer these criticisms we should look a little more closely at the development of Fo's career before passing on to examine precisely what are the bases of his popular theatre. Fo is a unique phenomenon in European drama: his work cannot be separated from his immense popularity as a performer. In the early 1960s his appearances on the television review *Canzonissima* literally stopped the traffic in Rome: taxi drivers lost most of their customers when the programme was being transmitted. By 1968 his company was celebrated throughout Italy, being familiar to theatre-goers through the commercial circuit, so it was a big step for him to break with this and decide to operate directly through Communist Party venues. His decision was not a sudden or arbitrary one: his motivation was clear.

It was getting more and more difficult to perform in a theatre where every feature, down to the division of seats into front stalls, rear stalls and gallery mirrored the class division. Where despite our best efforts we still remained the celebrated artists who every now and again came off their lofty social and professional pedestal. But above all to remain in the bourgeois theatre was becoming more and more contradictory bearing in mind

what we were beginning to understand at that time: that the most important decision for an intellectual was to come out of his gilded ghetto and place himself at the disposal of the movement.
(Valentini, *La storia di Dario Fo*, p. 104)

The difference between Fo's decision and that made by British theatre practitioners is marked. Arden and D'Arcy, and McGrath, work as class-outsiders wholly unfamiliar to their audiences in Ireland and Scotland; Fo was welcomed both as a celebrity and accepted as a member of the same class (his father was a railway worker). The decision of other British political writers – notably Bond, Brenton and Hare – to work through establishment channels, or – like Trevor Griffiths – to work through television may appear a more honest choice. Fo's sincerity and openness have never been in doubt. As the critic Elio Pagliarini has emphasised,

> What gives Fo his power, what prevents him from developing towards any form of artistic self-destruction, in the theoretically rigorous but abstract way which has characterised so many theatrical pioneers in the last few years, is his awareness of work in the theatre as a form of exchange. Whereby he puts in his contribution to receive in return something from the other side: from the reactions, the suggestions and the encouragements of the public, with whom he never loses contact for a moment.   (Ibid., p. 162)

This is where Fo scores: as creator and performer of his shows he is in a position to benefit critically from the exposure of his work to the public.

When in 1970 he and Franca Rame stopped working

directly with the Communist Party they were obliged for the first time to seek an audience on their own, unaided by either the *abbonamento* (subscription) scheme of the establishment theatres or the captive audiences of the *case del popolo*. They soon found theatre-goers, though never a permanent or satisfactory base. After four years of struggling to perform in inadequately equipped cinemas and converted warehouses in Milan, they finally occupied the Palazzina Liberty, a broken-down and abandoned building in the area once occupied by the Milanese wholesale fruit-and-vegetable market. There, from 1974 until they were forced to quit in 1982, they built up a new public for their original and popular shows. It is easy to romanticise and exaggerate their achievement. On the *Arena* television programme about Fo, Rob Walker speaks of them playing regularly to houses of 20,000. This is nonsense. In fact the Palazzina Liberty seated about 600, even though the warmth and interest generated among the audience led you to believe there were far more people present. Later, when the company played in circus tents – such as Teatro Tenda in Roma – the audience more than doubled. And later still they did perform at occupied factories and occasionally in sports stadia where the crowd reached the dimensions of one attending a football match or a pop show. Such is Fo's appeal. The audiences represent a cross-section of society. Again, the myth has grown up that Fo performs to mass audiences of workers. That has been so in the case of the shows at occupied factories. Even at the *case del popolo* in the late sixties the workers were outnumbered by students and party officials. A fair impression of the typical audience for Fo – certainly in the mid seventies – is given by this description of a performance of *Il Fanfani rapito*:

At the Piccolo [Giorgio Strehler's fashionable repertory theatre in Milan] you find the bourgeoisie, the cultural establishment and the prestigious critics. At the Palazzina you would find all the young thinking people of Milan: the kids who supported the referendum on divorce and those who were in favour of a direct confrontation with the Christian Democrats laughing and clapping at this fragmented, not completely roadworthy, gangster story of the Christian Democrat party and its secretary.

(Valentini, *La storia di Dario Fo*, p. 162)

Fo himself has emphasised,

In Italy popular theatre still exists . . . I have this popular tradition within me as part of my training, as a reflex. But you should note that there are hundreds of actors in Italy who 'sing' nonetheless and who when all's said and done, are 'naturalistic'. They are pompous, over emphatic naturalists. (*Red Notes*, 1983, p. 7)

Fo made these comments in discussing the popular theatrical tradition in Italy in relation to Brecht. His comments on Brecht's technique of epic theatre are particularly interesting in the context of Italian drama:

You see the German method of acting in that period, in all kinds of theatre, was a dreadful emphatic style, which was quite unacceptable. Everybody tended to chant or sing their parts. What reached the audience was no longer the argumentation of the drama, but the song/chant sound of that argumentation. So in order to achieve a levelling off, in order to restore a degree of naturalness, Brecht invented this technique.

(Ibid., pp. 6–7)

21

Much Italian theatre – the theatre of Vittorio Gassman, of Carmelo Bene, of Gabriele Lavia – is still very close in style to the 'sung' drama to which Fo refers. These three actors, all of whom direct their own work, continue the tradition of the *mattatore*: the powerful actor–manager whose overwhelming technique 'slays' the audience (a *mattatore* is literally a man who kills animals in a slaughterhouse). The nineteenth-century tradition of the star performer touring the country with his or her latest show – a tradition that reached its peak in the work of Eleonora Duse – has never really died out. As the actor and singer Luigi Proietti remarked in a review in 1984 (playing on the title of the Levi novel and Rosi film), 'Brecht si è fermato a Milano' (*Brecht Stopped in Milan*). Outside the work of Giorgio Strehler and Dario Fo his influence has been little felt in Italy.

Fo himself, however, is as much a *mattatore* as his celebrated contemporaries, even if his style of theatre is very different. Neither Britain nor America could ever have thrown up such a quintessentially Italian phenomenon. In another way too he is a part of a distinctively Italian theatre, which has always had a pronouncedly non-literary basis. You can count on the fingers of one hand the great international playwrights Italy has produced: there are just four – Goldoni, Pirandello, Eduardo de Filippo and Fo himself. Moreover, all of them have been concerned with the ambiguous distinction between theatre and life, concerned to explore the relationship between improvisation and the written text. Nor is it insignificant that they came from very different parts of Italy: from Venice, Sicily, Naples and Lombardy respectively. Italy has never known a real political and social unity. This has its disadvantages, but one great advantage is the pride in a regional culture such as Fo has manifested in his research into the artistic traditions of his own native Lombardy. Yet, if Italy has produced few international playwrights, there is no doubt that it is rich in *dramatists*: witness its strong tradition of musical theatre, which stretches from Monteverdi, through Bellini, Rossini and Verdi, to Puccini and Berio. This is the official theatrical culture of Italy, complemented by an equally rich tradition in the area of painting, sculpture and architecture. Though Fo dissociates himself from the establishment's view of art and the artist in his search for an alternative – and, for him, more vital – culture, he nevertheless belongs to a country with a magnificent heritage in every field relating to the dramatic medium.

In his rejection of an inflated theatrical style Fo has much in common with Brecht. His own definition of the epic style is clear and concise:

> The epic style derives from realism. But it is characterised by the self-aware detachment of the actor; the actor is critical of what he acts. He does not confine himself to conveying information, to telling something, and then letting the audience sort it all out. He seeks to provide the audience with the necessary data for a reading of the piece. (*Red Notes*, 1983, p. 6)

Fo's *bête noire* is the self-absorbed Method actor. In an interesting demonstration exercise he performed during the Riverside Studio workshops, he illustrated a significant corollary of his view of epic theatre: the importance of situation over character. Three volunteer actors were given a simple and clear line of action to play: they had to run on stage looking for something. They were to encounter a wall and a locked door both stage right and

23

stage left, and to try but fail to climb over the wall and kick down the door. Encountering a wall at the back of the stage, they were to turn, smile and start running, after a while coming to settle on their haunches, sad and disappointed. Before allowing the actors to perform this sequence of moves, Fo sent them away and informed the audience that the first actor had been in a fight in which he had stabbed someone. He has been cornered by the friends of the injured man, and when he cannot escape he sinks, pleadingly, to his knees. The second had had a row with his woman. She has left and he has gone in search of her. After searching in vain, he suddenly sees her approaching, but stops and sinks in his tracks when she meets another man, whom she kisses and goes off with. The third actor had been caught short and needs to find a lavatory. He searches desperately, then sees a green field. As he heads for it he realises he won't make it and sinks down defeated. When the three actors came to perform the actions they were in the eyes of the audience perfectly playing out the three situations Fo had described. Fo pointed out that the situation is more important than the actor's awareness of the part he is playing. Actors, he warned, all too readily, given the situation, go to excess in communicating the details of it and by so doing destroy its value. What the three actors had just achieved, he pointed out, was an example of epic acting. He concluded that 'to be epic is to be able to convey the situation before the finer details of it become apparent'. This technique is fundamental to his own style of performance, nowhere more clearly than in *Mistero buffo*.

Fo explained on *Arena* that he had come to realise that the basic element which was the key to his reanimation of popular theatrical forms was a skill in storytelling. The stories he had heard as a boy – usually from men involved in activities on the wrong side of the law – were, he later discovered, ancient tales that had been handed down orally over generations. The dramatic technique he learnt from these men was the basis of his success as a raconteur (in the reworking of medieval tales in *Mistero buffo* or of a Chinese fable in *La storia della tigre* [*The Story of the Tigress*, 1978]), as a crafter of farces and as a performer of *commedia dell'arte* routines. All these are popular theatrical forms which Fo has reinvested with his own skills – most notably, perhaps, the field of *commedia* acting about which he has this significant point to make:

> Given that these families [the celebrated Carissimi and Gelosi troupes of *commedia* players] existed, they were performing a certain kind of commedia which was generally conservative, and often downright reactionary in content (you should look at these pieces, see for yourselves). . . . There was, however, quite another tradition of comic actors within the Commedia dell'Arte, also professionals, who didn't frequent the courts and nobility, but worked in taverns, worked in town squares, worked in far lowlier circumstances. And it is no accident that their work has never been collected and published. They've never been catalogued. They've never been studied.  (*Red Notes*, 1983, p. 8)

He set about exploring what was known of this area, and his research – along with that of Strehler at the Piccolo Teatro in Milan – has been instrumental in rescuing *commedia* from the position of a quaint and charming curiosity and enabling it to become again a technique for exploring the social and political realities of life.

A typical example of Fo's skill as a *fabulatore* (storyteller) – and one which tells us a great deal about his own attitude to political theatre – is the story he published in the magazine *Rinascità* (29 October 1976) in answer to a Communist critic, Alberto Abruzzese, who had accused him of trying to establish a sort of utopian alternative without ever succeeding in formulating an articulate dramatic theory of his own. This story, 'Un teatro povero per i poveri' ('A poor theatre for the poor'), tells of how the lion, returning crestfallen one day after a vain attempt to capture the zebra, confesses his frustration to the lynx, who tells him not to meddle with such an animal but rather to find a cunning way of punishing it. Accordingly a council is convened and the lynx persuades the other animals that the zebra should be banished as a creature whose awkward way of running – part trot, part gallop, head down – reveals a total lack of elegance or style. Accordingly an edict is promulgated and affixed to every tree. The zebra, unable to read, gets a monkey to tell him what it says. On learning the truth he is furious and determines to reveal his elegance by copying the style of a circus horse. The other animals applaud, particularly the lion, who then in a bound jumps on the zebra and devours him. The final comment is left to the monkey: 'What a pity such a noble animal should be dead: he cared more about style than about saving his own skin. What an artist!'

Fo has never concerned himself with observing the rules – either those of the establishment or those of the conventional Left. He is an iconoclast, an artist who in the literal sense of the word wishes to subvert traditional values: to turn them upside-down. Yet there is method and purpose in his satire. He wishes to provoke. For this reason he regards *Anarchist* as his first – and possibly his most successful – attempt at what he regards as 'didactic theatre',

> which mustn't be documentary theatre, carefully organised, cold. A theatre which – for all the respect I have for Piscator – doesn't probe to the heart of things. It must be a vast mechanism that makes people laugh at what they see on stage, avoiding the liberating catharsis that can result from watching the drama enacted. A riotously funny, satirical, grotesque show doesn't permit you that liberation; when you laugh the sediment of anger stays inside you; the laughter doesn't allow you to be purged.
>
> (C. Valentini, *La storia di Dario Fo*, 1977, p. 136)

He has continued to provoke in many ways – in his presentation of Pope Bonifacio, for instance, as indeed in his subversion of religious values throughout *Mistero buffo*. Fo had been performing this for eight years in theatres before it was filmed for television in 1977, marking his return to the RAI studios after an absence of fifteen years. The production was condemned by the Vatican as 'the most sacrilegious performance ever broadcast since the invention of television', a censure which was followed by a cryptic telegram from Cardinal Vicar Ugo Poletti to Prime Minister Andreotti:

> Representative for countless citizens and organisations in Rome, express pain and protest at the desecratory and anti-cultural television programme: *Mistero buffo* by Dario Fo, to which profound humiliation added for the inconceivable vulgarity in a public transmission which vilifies the Italian nation in front of the world.
>
> (Valentini, *La storia di Dario Fo*, p. 175)

Pressure was put on the television authorities, but Mario Bubbico (described by Valentini as 'one of Fanfani's censors'), who was aiming to have Fo arrested and who had described him as an 'idealist trouble-maker, a liar, the mongoloid brother of Tati' (ibid.), was persuaded to back down.

No less a stir was caused by Fo's piece *Fedayn*, in which he put on stage a group of authentic Palestinian guerrillas who spoke and sang of their struggles against Zionism. These militant extremists from the PLO succeeded in offending not so much Jewish sympathies in Italy (which are not strong, as there is a healthy contempt for the alliance of American imperialism, and Zionism there) as the members of Al Fatah, the older and more moderate Palestinian guerrilla organisation. Perhaps the most disturbingly provocative of all Fo's theatrical devices, however, was the incorporation of what appeared to be outside interference into his drama *Guerra di popolo in Cile* (*People's War in Chile*, 1973), in order to suggest that a *coup d'état* like that organised by Pinochet could as easily take place in Italy. Fo's radio microphone appeared to be picking up police orders: shouting and gunfire was heard outside the theatre; and finally a police officer came in and read off a list of members of the extreme Left known to be in the house, stating that they were under arrest. The effect on audiences (it was repeated in several cities) varied from mass singing of the *Internationale* to panic: one man devoured several pages of his diary; another attempted to throw himself out of a window.

Fo's own brand of provocative theatre has inevitably brought reprisals: from censorship and prosecutions through to arrest and assault. After throwing an official out of a rehearsal in Sassari, Sardinia, in 1973, Fo was arrested and imprisoned for insulting conduct. He was released the next day after a massive national and international demonstration of solidarity. In March the same year, Franca Rame was abducted by a gang of fascists and slashed with razor blades. In a country famous for spectacular acts of violence – particularly in pursuit of revenge – it is perhaps not surprising that Fo and Rame have been subjected to such attacks. Italy has a habit of treating its rebel artists with a savagery that shocks the rest of Europe and America. Far more relentless was the legal persecution that dogged the career of the film director Pasolini, and far more terrible was his murder in Rome in 1975.

Fo's continuous involvement with Italian political issues, his attacks on such figures as Fanfani, Agnelli and Pope Wojtyła as well as his up-to-the-minute analysis of contemporary events, makes for acute problems when his plays are performed abroad. This is not helped by the fact that in much of his drama his characters speak either in slang or in dialect. 'Standard Italian' is an invention of the television era of the mass media. It takes as its norm not Tuscan but a hybrid language contemptuously dismissed by Pasolini as 'homogenised'. As a reaction to the imposition of this debased lowest common denominator of communication there has grown up a movement to protect and nurture the individual regional dialects of Italy – a movement to which both Fo and Pasolini have contributed through their employment of these dialects in their work. Both of these factors make the dramas of Fo uniquely difficult to translate: not only from the point of view of choosing the appropriate words, but, beyond this, from that of discovering an acting-language, a style of performance and a range of reference capable of preserving the spirit of the original while taking account of the new priorities consequent upon a shift of location.

Translation extends from the preparation of text (in Britain normally a two-part process, with one person making a literal translation and another adapting it) through the production style to the individual performances. The results – in the case of the professional British adaptations – vary: from the comparative fidelity to the original of *Female Parts* and *Trumpets and Raspberries* to the contrasted styles of *Anarchist* and *Can't Pay? Won't Pay!* reflecting decisions taken on the basis of quite different criteria. The style of *Anarchist* is brilliant, often recalling the comedy-of-manners idiom of Orton. But there is a danger here in that the implications of a sophistication alien to Fo move us in a crucial respect away from the language of popular theatre. The *Can't Pay? Won't Pay!* translation is much more prosaic and the characters have been given a British working-class manner of speaking (or, rather, what passes for working-class language amongst bourgeois theatre practitioners) which plays havoc with the Italian setting of the piece.

In an attempt to solve the problem created by this imbalance, a Midlands theatre group, Theatre Foundry, resorted in 1985 to the over-ingenious device of neutralising the language by employing the different regional accents of the cast: from Northern Irish through Yorkshire to Welsh. This resulted in a classic example of the tendency to set Fo's plays in some never-never land which bears little resemblance to reality – a tendency that inevitably blunts the cut of his satire. While this may be preferable to the Zeffirelli approach to the dramas of Eduardo de Filippo, where the actors spoke in a broad pseudo-Neapolitan which was considered deeply offensive, not least by the playwright himself, the real point is that Fo's dramas were inspired by and reflect very specific events and issues, divorced from which they become empty essays in style: he is the opposite of a universal writer. Whilst *Anarchist* had – at least initially – some relevance for the British scene, what can one say of *Trumpets and Raspberries*? The whole play depends on the audience's sense of outraged delight that Gianni Agnelli has been subjected to the indignities heaped on him in the play. So little did the figure of Agnelli mean to British audiences that Griff Rhys Jones was obliged to invent a digression within a digression in order to explain the significance of this figure: 'a bit like a cross between John DeLorean and the Duke of Kent'. This was ingenious – and has the great advantage of allowing the play to proceed without the need to invent a string of British references in place of those relating to Italian events. Yet the problem remained. Ultimately the play was shorn of its most important political content with the removal of all the lengthy references to Aldo Moro – another figure whose fate meant little to British audiences.

Absolute confusion of aim was paramount in the 1984 American adaptation of *Anarchist*, which – despite great publicity, the presence of Fo in the States for the first time and a star actor, Jonathan Pryce, in the lead – folded spectacularly within a week. It is not difficult to see why when one reads the adaptation, which substitutes for Fo's very precise up-to-date chronicle of Italian events a generalised critique of America, so sweeping (and celebratory) that it hurts no one and means nothing. It is set, for some inscrutable reason, in Rome, though all the references are to American institutions. From wisecracks about baseball and parking-tickets at the start it moves through attacks on Carter and Khomeini to a diatribe on the American judicial system, culminating in an in-discriminate review of American scandals as the adaptor, Richard Nelson, abandons any vestige of relevance to the original. New York audiences who had paid to see a work by Dario Fo were furious at being palmed off with a third rate, soft-centred American comedy (satire would be too strong a word). Since the translator keeps the US rights to the play for twenty years, even though Fo has banned any further performances of the adaptation, a crazy situation worthy of his own theatre exists which one is tempted to see as part of a continuing plot to prevent his work from being seen in America.

In Britain the unsatisfactory nature of the adaptations leads to a curious 'knock-on' effect. Lack of consideration of the social and political circumstances in which the works were born leads to an undue and inaccurate emphasis on style. This was particularly marked in a recent production of *Anarchist* at the Birmingham Repertory Theatre. When interviewed, the director, Derek Nicholls, expressed the surprise that all too frequently greets the suggestion that an adaptation of Fo differs radically from the Italian original and pointed out that to him the word 'farce' (Fo's term) was an inaccurate description of the work, which he felt exhibited a pot-pourri of styles and was akin to Jarrry's *Ubu roi*. In fairness one can see how that might be his reading of the adaptation. Accordingly he exaggerated the farcical elements and introduced new 'political' material expressly written for the occasion by that Shadwell of dramatists, David Edgar, in order to remedy the balance and introduce a seriousness supposedly lacking in the original. In subsequent chapters we shall analyse precisely how Fo's farce works and how the adaptation has interfered with the precision of his savagely comic mechanism by opting for what Fo himself has called 'solutions which are more exclusively comic'. For instance, the careful series of gags which are primed to explode so as to emphasise the serious political issues in the final part of *Anarchist* are defused in the adaptation when, instead of appearing in his last disguise wearing merely false moustache, false hand and eye-patch, the Maniac is '*outrageously costumed. He wears false moustache, glasses, wild wig, wooden leg, false hand, eye-patch, carries a crutch.*' By the time the play had reached Birmingham the character was sporting red wig, crutch, wooden leg, Sherlock Holmes pipe and magnifying glasses, green tartan cape, deerstalker and stuffed parrot.

Far more offensive, however, because so presumptuous and typical of a certain wing of British political theatre, was the feeling that it was necessary to introduce a spurious topicality into the play. Again the cue for this comes from the adaptation, which – employing entirely the wrong kind of improvisation – at one point has this stage direction: '*Gives detailed examples of political murder and state repression in Britain.*' This is the signal for the self-righteous left-wing dramatist to let his hair down, and Edgar obliges with a list including

> How many more Russian spies are knocking back the Chateau Whatitsface at Buckingham Palace? Why does Anthony Blunt get off scot free while poor old Geoffrey Prime gets creamed? Wrong class, wrong station. Same as why Sarah Tisdall gets six months for telling the Guardian what Cecil Parkinson told Sarah Keays, and what's the betting he's back in the cabinet before the next election?

This particular effusion was greeted in Birmingham by appreciative applause on at least one occasion. Fo's carefully judged satirical provocation had been turned into what is the bane of so much British political theatre: smug, self-congratulatory celebration.

It may seem both harsh and unfair to berate adaptations of dramas which initially have a flexible text. But the complex metamorphosis through which Fo guides his work is always subject to the most careful scrutiny. If it seems that the prospects for worthwhile productions of his work abroad are thin (and it must be pointed out that rarely does anyone else perform his plays in Italy!) this impression must be corrected by a recent development: the emergence of Franca Rame as an ostensibly more equal partner in the relationship. She has always starred with Fo and has been responsible for the administration of their company. But, since the appearance of her monologues collected under the title *Tutta casa, letto e chiesa* (*It's All Home, Bed and Church* known in Britain as *Female Parts*), which was first seen in 1977 and revised in 1981 (the version familiar in Britain), she has brought women's issues more urgently to the fore in the partnership. In 1977 she said,

> Before our retreat from the official theatre circuit my characters, the female characters created by Dario, were in effect decorative, hangers on, though they had their say and argued about things albeit in a mad sort of way. Then in 1968 we broke with all that. The mother of Michele Lu Lanzone is an old woman, desperate and suffering like a madonna beneath the cross; the main character in *Legami pure* is a grey-haired fifty-year old woman who has been destroyed and is full of anger. All of them are characters divorced from the more superficially attractive figures I'd once portrayed.   (Valentini, *La storia di Dario Fo*, p. 173)

Earlier the same year, Rame had presented another one-woman show: *Parliamo di donne*, an anthology of pieces concerned with precisely these more powerful figures. In all these pieces, and a number of later ones – a monologue by a woman who has been raped (*Lo stupro*, 1983), a lengthy narration by a mother who has discovered that her son has been arrested for terrorist activities and visits him in prison (*La madre*, 1983), and the one-act two-hander *Coppia aperta*, (*The Open Couple*, 1983) – Rame has been instrumental in bringing to the forefront sharply contrasted facets of political oppression in relation to women. Her monologues – partly because of their stark, straightforward expository style, and their focus on one character's predicament, and partly because of their theme, which is more universally applicable than so much of Fo's drama – have received more authentic performances in Britain than any of the team's other work to date.

This has in turn produced a tension within Fo and Rame's relationship. The tension was particularly marked in *Quasi per caso una donna, Elisabetta* (*Elizabeth, Almost by Accident a Woman* 1984), which, despite the performance of Franca Rame in the title role, advanced neither the feminist cause nor the reputation of the partnership. One of the drawbacks of Fo's brand of deliberately throwaway theatre is that at times it is capable of producing trash. Such was the case with this play, an embarrassing exercise in pseudo-history revolving round Elizabeth I's supposed twin obsessions: her fading beauty and the belief that she is the endless victim of Shakespeare's satire. The show purports to be about the role of the subversive political writer, but Shakespeare does not appear; rather, Fo turns up in the unlikely disguise of a coarse female quack, La Donnazza, renowned for her miraculous beauty treatments. Hence Elizabeth is subjected to endless indignities such as an attempt to increase the size of her breasts through being stung by bees, and the audience to scatological humour – as at the end of Act I, when the Queen pisses herself. Fo dubiously claimed contemporary relevance for the piece in the parallel between the ability to turn Queen's evidence – an invention credited to Elizabeth's minister Walsingham – and dalla Chiesa's encouragement of repentant terrorists to grass on their comrades in return for lighter sentences. Rame sailed through the play – which robbed her of all dignity as a woman – with total contempt (at the first performance she was prompted all the way through by means of a radio microphone). On the last performance (the one I saw) she seemed determined to get through the play as quickly as possible and Fo to upstage her – in drag – at every conceivable point.

But Fo recognises his mistakes. The final performances projected for Turin were scrapped and *Mistero buffo* substituted. On the announcement of the change of programme the 'House Full' sign went up within the day. Fo's success was followed by Rame's – in a series of performances of *Coppia aperta*, with the two latest monologues forming the second half of the programme. Who knows what may happen to *Elisabetta*? Given Fo and Rame's skill in adapting their work to the interests and needs of their audience, they could yet turn the text into something more valuable. They have proved over and over again that they possess that most indispensable of all qualities to a healthy and popular political theatre: flexibility.

# 2
# Farce and Satire

Il Comico, scavando nella tradizione popolare, ne assimila maniere e techniche che divantano sue, sia quando scrive per il teatro che quando agisce sulla scena. Quando scrivevo le farse, per esempio, mi ero reso conto concretamente che non c'è vero teatro che non sia teatro di situazione. Ogni azione teatrale nasce da una situazione scenica pregnante di sviluppi di azione. Il dialogo è solo uno degli strumenti per esprimere questi sviluppi. . . . Il teatro che vuole basarsi su di un dialogo autonomo dallo sviluppo di un'azione, che non è espressivo di un'azione potenziale, non è teatro, è letteratura.

[The comic artist, drawing his inspiration from the tradition of popular theatre, takes over its habits and techniques which he then makes his own, whether he writes for the theatre or appears on the stage. When I was writing my farces, for instance, I realized very clearly that there was no real theatre that wasn't a

37

theatre of situation. Every theatrical action is born from a stage situation capable of giving rise to new twists of plot. The dialogue is just one of the means of explaining these complications. . . . The theatre that wants to base itself on dialogue that is independent of the development of plot, that doesn't give scope for further action, isn't theatre, it's literature.]

(*Dario Fo parla di Dario Fo*, [Lerici: Cosenza, 1977] pp. 21–2)

The most powerful political weapon in Fo's theatrical armoury is farce. In the introduction to the Italian edition of *Non si paga, non si paga!* (*Can't Pay? Won't Pay!*) he argues that his theatrical collective, La Comune, has made a kind of prophecy – nothing magical, he adds, but a careful application of logic which through inquiry and analysis tests belief and puts Marxist ideology into practice. Referring to Gramsci he asks, 'But is it possible to create a farce using this "philosophy of praxis"?', and citing Mao, who argued that it is necessary always to doubt in order not merely to destroy but also to build, he concludes,

We too are convinced that in laughter, in the grotesque humour of satire resides the maximum expression of doubt, the most valid agent of reason. That's why as means and instrument of our work as theatre practitioners in the service of the class struggle we have chosen farce which is the theatrical form invented by the people to cut through the putrefying body monopolised by the establishment with savage unsparing force. That putrefying body which is bourgeois culture. (*Non si paga,* 1974, pp. 3–4)

Farce, according to Fo, is an ancient dramatic form, traceable to the Greeks and much used in classical Rome, as well as by the entertainers of the Middle Ages. It represents a precise application of logic and at the same time leaves room for improvisation; and it is particularly in this context that we can appreciate the full meaning of the term 'improvisation' for Fo. Improvisation does not imply an undisciplined ad-libbing, a following of whatever whim or inclination the actor is drawn to. Rather – like the jazz musician – the performer is required to know his material so well that he is able to mould and adapt it to changes of circumstance, thereby extending its basic potential in new variations, never obscuring or ignoring the central theme. It is precisely because British adapters, directors and actors have not understood this fundamental concept that his plays have been travestied in Britain, their careful structure – representing an extension of political theory into theatrical practice – ignored.

We therefore face a curious problem in examining the three farces – *Accidental Death of an Anarchist, Can't Pay? Won't Pay!* and *Trumpets and Raspberries* – which have been and continue to be the most frequently performed of Fo's dramas in Europe and America. It is the problem of how to discuss the *text*. In the case, notably, of the British versions of both *Can't Pay? Won't Pay!* and *Accidental Death of an Anarchist* what an audience sees on stage is often a very far cry from what Fo (at any stage in the work's genesis) actually wrote. This is not necessarily in itself a bad thing – there are aspects of the British adaptation of *Accidental Death of an Anarchist* which in their wit and vibrant theatricality match anything in Fo – but it makes the critic's task a difficult one. Either he discusses the originals (thereby forcing his readers who do not speak Italian to take what he says on trust) or he discusses those adaptations with which his readers are familiar (and which quite often depart radically from what Fo wrote). We are dealing here, moreover, with a living artist whose work is of vital interest outside Italy. If he were merely a phenomenon of his own country, a difficult asset to export – as, it could be argued, is more the case with Eduardo de Filippo – he would be far less interesting and possess little more than curiosity value for non-Italians. It would be misleading to argue that Fo's dramas have a universal appeal, though the skill of his meticulously contrived plots is appreciable and appealing in a variety of contexts. The theatrical mechanism in each case, however, is related very specifically to a political issue, grounded in a precise historical context and designed to function as a device for opening up discussion through analysis and questioning of fact. There has all too often been a tendency to seize on the skilful dramatic form, set it in motion and assume it will function as a satiric agent for provoking debate in a very different context. But, unless the balance between fact and fiction, between seriousness and farce, between tragedy and comedy, is respected and maintained, there is a real danger of losing the essential meaning and thereby falling into a form of safe, comforting political celebration.

Fo's farces are not safe. He does not see the aim of his theatre as one of liberating his audience through the purgative force of comedy. It could be argued that the function of comedy is to 'purge with delight the melancholy of the audience' (to borrow a phrase from Guarini). Fo would be more in agreement with Umberto Eco, however, who in his brilliant reconstruction of Aristotle's theory in *The Name of the Rose* sees, by contrast, the dangerous potential of laughter as a destroyer of accepted faith. It is precisely because Fo – like Edward Bond – does not accept traditional values (either of the establishment or of established Marxist theory) but rather is concerned to put speculation and theory to the test that he lives out in the theatre Gramsci's fundamental approach to discovering a valid – because practical – Marxism. His dramas, and particularly his farces, are an equivalent of Bond's extension of epic theatre into an area where the play is capable of 'dramatising the analysis'.

It will, therefore, be the aim of this chaper to examine those features of *Accidental Death of an Anarchist, Can't Pay? Won't Pay!* and *Trumpets and Raspberries* which are common to the original dramas and their British adaptations. We shall see how the mechanisms of farce work not only to provoke laughter but also as instruments for opening up political issues. In Chapter 3 a more detailed comparison of the originals with the British versions will be undertaken, to explore in greater depth those skills which are peculiar to Fo and which have proved difficult to recapture in translation.

## 'Accidental Death of an Anarchist'

This farce, first performed in December 1970, was grounded in very specific, disturbing political reality. A year previously, on 12 December 1969, a bomb exploded in the Agricultural Bank in Piazza Fontana in Milan, killing sixteen people and injuring a hundred. This was one of the many bomb outrages which marked the volatile political situation in Italy in the late sixties and the seventies. They were to reach their bloody climax in the tragedy at Bologna station in 1980, and we gain some idea of the climate of tension from the fact – it is no exaggeration as quoted in the play – that within the twelve months prior to the creation of *Anarchist* there had been 173 bomb attacks in Italy. So serious was the situation that in the late seventies the head of the Italian police force, General Alberto dalla Chiesa, developed a tactic of granting immunity or reduced sentences to terrorists who were prepared to confess and thus incriminate their colleagues. Some indication of the scope of the problem may also be gleaned from the way in which the Italian language – so skilful in recycling its vocabulary – came up with a whole series of terms for such terrorists, according to their relative willingness to co-operate; for example, the *pentito* was prepared to co-operate unreservedly with the police, the *dissociato* admitted his error but refused to 'grass', and the *irriducibile* refused to budge in his convictions. The situation was very different from that of the IRA in Britain, where the ethical and political implications of terrorism are much more clear-cut. Italy has suffered from a complex double strain of terrorism, the so-called *trama nera* and *trama rossa*, representative of the right wing and left wing respectively, with fascist ideology opposing that of the Red Brigades. Indeed, 'ideology' is a term much more appropriately applied to terrorism in Italy than to its counterpart in Britain. Because of the difficulty of apportioning blame (or 'responsibility', as the IRA prefers to call it) two theories of terrorism were developed in the late seventies: that of the *opposti estremismi* – two extremist factions fighting for power in the country; and that of the *grande vecchio* – the international puppeteer manipulating all the agents involved in order to gain control.

After the bombing in the Milan bank, a young anarchist, Giuseppe Pinelli, was arrested, along with a ballet dancer, Pietro Valpreda. Valpreda remained in prison for ten years (publishing, not unlike Gramsci before him, his prison diaries). Pinelli was less fortunate: he was killed when his body flew out of the fourth floor of the police headquarters where he was being interrogated. When the trial of the accused anarchists finally came to an end – ten years later, at Catanzaro – three fascists were condemned as perpetrators of the bombing. Fo was not the only person who mistrusted the charges against Pinelli and Valpreda in 1969. The extra-parliamentary left-wing newspaper *Lotta continua* accused the inspector in charge, Calabrese, of causing Pinelli's death, and he in turn instigated a lawsuit against the paper. It was whilst the case against *Lotta continua* was being tried in Milan that Fo decided to mount his play. Each performance incorporated the latest court findings, whilst Fo and his collective were further assisted by lawyers and journalists who provided them with photocopies of unpublished evidence and documents relating to the judicial inquiry into the case. A similar situation was exploited in Britain when the Royal Shakespeare Company in 1970 dramatised the day-to-day court proceedings in the *Oz* trial. But there is a world of difference between the British preoccupation with the matter of censorship and Fo's involvement with a far more complex and dangerous political issue.

The extent of this involvement and the consequent force and seriousness of the play are seen in the note Fo wrote for the Birtish edition of the play:

Our intervention, as the 'La Comune' collective, was therefore, above all, an exercise in counter-information. Using authentic documents – and complete transcripts of the investigations carried out by the various judges as well as police reports – we turned the logic and truth of the facts on [their] head. But the great and provocative impact of this play was determined by its theatrical form: rooted in tragedy, the play became farce – the farce of power. The public who came to the theatre – progressive students, workers, but also large numbers of the lower middle class – was overwhelmed by the grotesque and apparently mad way in which the play worked. They split their sides laughing at the effects produced by the comical and at the same time satirical situations. But as the performance went on, they gradually came to see that they were laughing the whole time at real events, events which were criminal and obscene in their brutality: crimes of the state.

(Introduction to *Accidental Death of an Anarchist*, 1980, p. iii)

Fo goes on to stress that the way in which this mixture of seriousness and farce caused the grins on the audience's face to freeze and turn 'into a kind of *grand guignol* scream which had nothing liberating about it'. We are reminded of the technique of another highly subversive dramatist, Christopher Marlowe, and notably of his play *The Jew of Malta*, which T. S. Eliot famously and aptly described with the phrase 'savage farce'.

In *Anarchist*, Fo invents a central character, the Maniac, in whose apparent madness there is throughout a sound method. It is the Maniac's seemingly insane logic which is instrumental in unmasking the criminal folly of the police in their attempts to cover up their actions. The Maniac's persistent ridiculing of the police's shaky case through forcing them – in his disguise as the investigating magistrate – to re-enact the events and then subsequently to contradict themselves in explaining the anarchist's 'suicidal' action is a clever dramatic device whereby Fo can dismantle the whole tissue of half-truths and non-sequiturs by which the authorities, through careful manipulation of the media, managed to convince the public that the Milan bombing had been a planned action by left-wing extremists.

The Maniac reveals his lunatic logic in action from the start, one which is designed to make the police look fools. When they accuse him of deliberately misrepresenting himself through the information on his visiting cards he has an answer ready:

> Look . . . a minute . . . the punctuation changes the whole emphasis of the sentence. After the comma, the reader – your good self – takes a short mental breath thus changing the intentionality. You see? So, the sentence should read . . . 'Professor Antonio Rabbia' . . . comma . . . capital 'P' 'Psychiatrist'!!! Full stop. 'Formerly' . . . comma . . . 'Lecturer at the University of Padua'!!! You see, read correctly only an arsehole would swallow it.   (*Anarchist*, p. 3)

His own ingenious manipulation of language is the perfect weapon against the distortion of the facts perpetrated by the police and the media. After being thrown out of the police station – unconvicted for the seventeenth time – he returns and takes advantage of a phone conversation to reappear in the guise of the one character he has always wanted to play: a judge. As a certified psychotic suffering, according to his medical report, from 'histrionic mania', he is compelled constantly to play the parts of a whole range of characters; his masquerading as Professor *Rabbia* (the word means madness in Italian) is only the prologue to what will become a rapidly escalating sequence of impersonations.

As the Judge – Professor Marco Maria Malipiero, first

councillor to the High Court, a role he is unwittingly assigned by Inspector Pissani over the telephone – he is able to run rings round the police in their vain attempt to make sense of their confused and fabricated evidence. Before the Maniac is let loose on the police in his first proper disguise, Fo takes several cunning swipes at the judiciary by having the Maniac point out the irony of the fact that, whilst most workers are finished, pensioned off, at sixty, a judge at that age is just beginning his career:

> Take your lathe operator – touch of the shakes, couple of minor accidents, out to grass. Coal miner, bit of silicosis and he's fucked at fifty. . . . But the frailer and feebler judges get, the more they are elevated to superior and powerful positions. Oh yes, that's the job for me. 'Fifty years for you, thirty years for you. Case dismissed. Council can come and corrupt me in my chambers.' (Ibid., p. 4)

His judge, however, is no fool. He forces the police literally to re-enact the events of the night the anarchist dies, with hilarious consequences, and gets them to admit they completely misled the suspect so as to browbeat him into a confession:

> You arrest a free citizen, hold him beyond the legal time limit, and then traumatise him by telling him you have absolute proof that he is a bomber which you later state you didn't have at all, tell him you'll make sure he loses his job, and in spite of three sworn affidavits from witnesses who positively identify this woebegone railwayman as their card-playing colleague in Naviglia you tell him his alibi has collapsed. (Ibid., p. 16)

This is the precise aim of Fo's 'counter-information': here, despite the ironic tone of the accusation (one which, it must be pointed out, is emphasised much more strongly in the English translation) we should be in no doubt of the serious aim of the play – to expose the real facts of the case.

The Maniac as Judge now terrorises the police into an even more ironic re-enacting of previous events: they are put in the position of the anarchist as the Judge invents the idea of the state using them as scapegoats 'to salvage what is left of the mangled reputation of its police force'. It is an irony which, as we shall see, is blunted in the English adaptation, though, as the police are forced to the window and told by the Maniac to jump, the chilling reversal of the situation is inescapable. After this the Judge changes tack to help the police, supporting their alteration of the time of the interrogation (moved back four hours) in order to exculpate them from any responsibility in the anarchist's 'leap' to his death. Quite the opposite effect is produced, as the police struggle helplessly to circumvent the inevitable. Fo's ridicule is intensified here as the attempts to present the police as the heroes of the occasion lead to further satire.

The police are encouraged to invent more and more details of their kindness and humanity – from giving the anarchist a piece of chewing gum to recalling their childhood love of playing with trains through to their communal singing with the accused man. Fo extracts an immense amount of humour from all this, a technique which recalls that of Orton in *Loot*, who causes his brutal policeman, Truscott, to masquerade as an employee of the Water Board, acting with urbanity and charm yet scarcely able to repress his urge to beat the life out of the suspects, Hal and Dennis. When the Judge intimates that

the police may have used physical violence their insistence
that they were interrogating him 'lightheartedly' leads to
a lengthy piece of ironic description worthy of Orton as
the Judge expresses relief that the 'shrieks and screams
and slappings and loud thuds' which kept him awake when
he was staying next to the police station in Bergamo were
in fact harmless:

> Naturally I assumed as any citizen who reads the papers
> and watches TV would, that these were the sounds of
> suspects being beaten under interrogation by brutal
> country coppers. All too clearly now I can see how
> mistaken my impressions were. Those shrieks I heard
> were shrieks of laughter, the screams were screams of
> merriment and mirth accompanied by thigh-slapping
> convulsions of humorous hysteria.   (*Anarchist*, p. 24)

Already Fo's topsy-turvy techniques are beginning to
escalate the play into farce. They are carried a stage
further when the Maniac, having suggested that it would
be greatly in their favour if the police could prove
that they had tried to stop the anarchist from jumping,
encourages them into wilder and wilder inventions. At the
constable's suggestion that he grabbed the anarchist's foot
with the result that his shoe came off, the Maniac points
out the inconvenient fact that the anarchist was wearing
both shoes when his body was recovered, which leads to
this extension of the zany logic:

> PISSANI   (*beside himself with panic*): Very well.
> Obviously one of the suspect's shoes must have been
> too big for him – so, not having an insole to hand, he
> had previously put a smaller shoe on inside the bigger
> one which came off in the constable's hand! Or one

foot was considerably smaller than the other and the same means was employed to even up the feet for cosmetic reasons!! (*Pause.* PISSANI *looks manically triumphant.* MANIAC *sits back to enjoy the scene.*)

SUPERINTENDENT: Two shoes on one foot?

PISSANI: Precisely.

CONSTABLE It's not as mad as it sounds, sir.

SUPERINTENDENT: It's fucking deranged.    (Ibid., p. 26)

Fo's ridicule of police logic can be carried no further, and at this point the farce undergoes a further development with the entry of the journalist Maria Feletti. This character is based on Camilla Cederna, a reporter from the weekly magazine *L'espresso* who had been responsible for exposing some uncomfortable facts about the Pinelli affair. With her arrival the Maniac is forced to play another role – a disguise within a disguise – so as not to be recognised as a judge, and chooses to be Captain Marcantonio Piccini of the forensic department. Fo has deliberately organised the drama so that the most serious part of the play – the lengthy discussions which follow between Feletti and the Maniac and which expose (as Cederna had done) the wider corruption of the establishment – precisely coincides with the most comic: the inevitable realisation by Bertozzo that the forensic expert is the Maniac and the attempts of the others to silence him on the mistaken assumption that he is the Judge in disguise. This is the province of pure farce, the consequence of the escalating series of impersonations and misunderstandings which have developed so far in the play.

And it is precisely here that the British adaptation parts company most completely with the original, cutting a large number of the lengthier discussions and at the same time inventing a whole sequence of added comic gags. The effect is to diminish the careful balance of the serious and the comic in the play and to defuse the subtle mechanism Fo has invented to explode here the distortions and misconceptions of current beliefs about terrorists' activities. Two carefully handled comic techniques underpin the play's satiric force at this point. One is the way in which the audience anticipates Bertozzo's gradual realisation of the identity of the Maniac and then looks on delightedly as he is silenced by the others. The frantic chase which is set up in the British version is less effective than the sequence of gags in the original, whereby the Maniac is taken to one side, forced to pretend to make a phone call, and then subjected to a series of attempts to shut him up. First the receiver is stuffed in his mouth. This proves ineffective, so a rubber stamp is used instead. When he still tries to spill the beans, his mouth is sealed with tape and he is finally injected with a sedative. Whereas in the British version the fast series of entrances and exits, coupled with pratfalls and false directions, distracts attention from the discussion between Feletti and the Maniac, in the original Bertozzo is literally silenced so that the centrally serious issue is never effectively upstaged by the comedy.

Another technique of the skilful farceur is lost in the British adaptation. When the Maniac disguises himself as the forensic expert he goes offstage and returns to create an impression:

> *He* [the Superintendent] *dries up as he turns to come face to face with the* MANIAC. MARIA FELETTI *and* PISSANI *have risen to their feet and stare openmouthed, as does the* CONSTABLE. *The* MANIAC *is outrageously costumed. He wears false moustache, glasses, wild wig, wooden*

*leg, false hand, eye-patch, carries a crutch.*
(Anarchist, p. 30)

In at least one British production (see Chapter 1) he also had a parrot on his shoulder. Fo, however, knows how to pull his punches, to keep things in reserve as a comedian. (Moreover, in the original, he has yet another disguise in store.) The Maniac in his version changes quickly at the back of the stage and when he turns floors only the Superintendent. He wears only the false moustache, the false hand and the eye-patch. The moustache is crucial to his fooling of Bertozzo later; the false hand and eye-patch will also figure significantly in the comedy.

Fo uses all these props tellingly. There is not a gag in the long final scene which is not there to underline a serious point. The rhythm of the scene is calculated to control the audience response as they are jerked by comic dislocation into a fuller awareness of serious issues. Immediately after the discussion of when the anarchist fell, leading into praise of the Italian flexibility over time, the Maniac's eye pops out (*Anarchist*, p. 75). The description of how the police inadvertently allowed the anarchist to fall is underlined by the Inspector tripping on the eye (p. 76). As Feletti emphasises the significance of the verdict of the inquiry that the death was 'accidental' rather than suicide, as the police claim, the Maniac swallows the glass eye (p. 77). During a lengthy attack (a page and a half in the Italian; cut in the British version) on the class bias shown by the judiciary in listening favourably to wealthy industrialists, the Maniac reveals for the first time his wooden leg (p. 82); immediately following, Bertozzo enters. When Feletti draws blood with her incriminating revelation that the police infiltrated the anarchist group with fascist informers, the Maniac makes

her shake his hand, whereupon it comes off (p. 90).

In emphasising the particular comic skills of Fo as a writer of cunningly constructed farce we have inevitably strayed a little into what will be the province of the next chapter: the British adaptations. But it is vital at this stage in our analysis of his work that we do not underrate the precise techniques whereby he employs the most popular of theatrical genres for advancing his no less carefully considered political viewpoint.

### 'Can't Pay? Won't Pay!'

This farce, first performed in 1974, also grew out of an urgent response to contemporary events. A form of civil disobedience that expressed itself in *autoriduzione* or appropriation began to spread through Italy. People refused to pay the rising prices for food, electricity, transport and so on occasioned by a crisis in the economy, and were prepared to pay only what they considered to be fair. Unemployment was dramatically on the increase, exacerbating the situation. In Britain, a society which exerts draconian fines and inflicts prison sentences for petty theft or evasion of fares on public transport, such a protest is scarcely conceivable. There is thus a pronounced irony in the fact that *Can't Pay? Won't Pay!* enjoyed a longer West End run than any of Fo's other dramas to be played there, and that its London audiences were predominantly composed of middle-class theatregoers – members of precisely that class that plays the largest part in maintaining this savagely punitive system. As Truscott sardonically comments in Orton's *Loot*, 'There is one crime the state considers worse than murder . . . the stealing of public money.'

In fact, as we shall observe, the British version of the play is at a considerable remove from what Fo wrote, retaining none of the political relevance and savage bite of the original. The mechanisms of farce are by and large retained in this adaptation (by Bob Walker), but they are no longer integrated with the serious issues which inspired the play in the first place. This lets the audience off the hook, which the original certainly does not. As Fo emphasises in his introduction to the Italian edition, the play takes as its subject the most basic of all farce themes – hunger:

> As in the old popular (they would be best termed ancient) farces from Naples and the Veneto, the starting point, the motivation of the drama, is hunger. In order to solve the problem of appetite (an atavistic need) the instinctive solution is initially to look after number one, but this changes to a desire to operate collectively, to get organised and struggle together not merely to exist but to live in a just world.
>
> (*Non si paga, non si paga!*, 1974, p. 4)

Hence the story Fo tells is seriously concerned with 'civil disobedience' as a 'new form of strike action. A type of strike in which at last it's the boss and only the boss who has to pay.'

The play skilfully operates through a seemingly improvisatory structure which sets up a conflict of viewpoint between the upholder of convention (Giovanni) and the more radical critics and rebels (Antonia, Luigi and the Police Sergeant). Cunningly, Fo, the actor, gives himself unlimited potential to poke fun, though here the mockery functions in precisely the opposite way from that in *Accidental Death of an Anarchist*: it actually serves to strengthen not what the Fo character, Giovanni, upholds, but what the others are saying. We take sides against Giovanni and realise that all these arguments, reasonable and law-abiding as they may appear, are misplaced and consequently worthless. A comparison may be made here with the old BBC comedy series *Steptoe and Son* and *Till Death Us Do Part*, in both of which an old reactionary was allowed to pay out endless lengths of prejudice which serves only to strangle him and his view. In Fo's play, the fact that Giovanni is a Communist only makes the irony more telling. There is also an interesting parallel with another British television comedy series, *Shine on Harvey Moon*, where the dull and normal Harvey was endlessly coming up against the more advanced views of his girl friend, Frieda, and his estranged wife, Rita (a part played with consummate skill by Maggie Steed, who starred in the hugely successful West End run of *Can't Pay? Won't Pay!*).

Fo's play functions through two dramatic devices: the farce structure and the clash of values between Giovanni and his wife, best friend and new acquaintance, the Police Sergeant. It is not insignificant that *Can't Pay? Won't Pay!* is one of the few plays he has written that Fo has seen fit to revive (partly as a result of successful productions abroad, notably at the Berliner Ensemble and in London). He remounted and reworked the play in 1980, further extending the limitless potential the dramatic structure offers for comment on contemporary political events. Discussions on the Pope (the recently elected Wojtyła ), the strikes in Poland and the situation at Fiat, where 24,000 redundancies were announced (an action Fo described as a 'massacre', in effect a deliberate continuation of the one at Bologna station) were worked into the new version. In his confrontations with the other characters Giovanni was made to act as devil's advocate to Fo's criticism of the Pope, which has grown and developed – notably in *Mistero buffo* – ever since, and here focused on the contradiction between the Pope's support for the striking workers in Gdansk and disapproval of similar industrial action in Italy. A cunningly disarming theatrical strategy was used to imply that the Vatican was supporting the Polish workers' organisation Solidarity with the assistance of the CIA in order to oppose Communism in the Eastern bloc.

The play plots the gradual but inevitable conversion of Giovanni to the more enlightened views of his wife and his friend, whose more direct and straightforward responses to the economic situation are matched by the far more sophisticated and sophistical arguments of the 'red' policeman. Things, in fact, are not what they seem in the play, neither in Giovanni's private life nor in the world outside, and he has to come to terms with this. Through Antonia's and his attempts to hide the consequences of their actions we – the audience – are drawn vicariously into their world and our own neat assumptions are challenged.

It is Antonia's 'appropriation' of goods in a supermarket and her fear of telling Giovanni the truth about this that initiates the deception which sets the farcical ball rolling. Antonia gets her friend Margherita to stuff food under her coat, and, when Giovanni sees her swollen shape, Antonia – true to the best traditions of farce – is forced into the expedient of inventing an explanation: she says Margherita is pregnant. This comes as a surprise to the conventional Giovanni, who is sure her husband, Luigi, his best friend, would have told him. Later, when the women leave for the hospital after the Police Inspector has explained that Margherita need not worry since a new technique of transplanting unborn babies into another woman's womb will guarantee the safety of her child, Giovanni is left in the house. This is the second time in the act that he has been left alone, and on both occasions Fo uses soliloquy to expand the basic theme of the play.

On the first occasion Giovanni, believing his wife has only been able to afford dog food, when in fact she snatched the tin in her haste in the supermarket, is forced to consider eating it. He has already shown his distaste for the other items Antonia grabbed in confusion: millet for canaries and frozen rabbit heads, but he is stopped from going to eat out when Antonia informs him she has no money. The economic situation is serious but the humour Fo extracts from it is richly comic, strongly recalling Zanni's hunger, a part of *Mistero buffo* in which the poor fool is so desperately hungry that he is forced to *imagine* what he will eat, finally attempting to devour himself:

> Blimey, I'm starving. (*He picks up the tin.*) 'Supermeat for dogs.' Homogenised, tasty. Wonder what it tastes like? Hello, she's lost the key as usual. Wait a minute. Screwtop. (*He opens the tin.*) Doesn't smell too bad. Bit like pickled jam with a soupçon of truffled kidneys, laced with cod liver oil. A dog'd be a madman to eat this crap. Think I'll have a drop of lemon on top against the cholera. (*Can't Pay? Won't Pay!*, 1982, p. 9)

Left alone again later in the act, he discovers the olives which have dropped out of the plastic bag that Margherita had stuffed under her coat and which was torn in the haste to get away. Again his ignorance and gullibility – in sharp contrast to Antonia's resourcefulness and ingenuity – are exploited as he tries to work out the origin of the water and its connection with the olives:

Blimey, all this water! But what a strange smell, like vinegar . . . yeah, sort of brine, that's it. Hello? . . . what's this now, an olive? Olives and brine? I can't believe it! No, I must be crazy. Olives don't come into it! Oh look, here's another one! Two olives? If it wasn't for their rather uncertain origin, I'd eat them . . . I'm so hungry! I almost feel like making myself some millet soup. It might even be good. I'll stick in two stock cubes . . . a head of onion.   (Ibid., p. 20)

In fact he sticks in the offensive and offending frozen rabbits' heads, which does not stop the unsuspecting Luigi from tasting the result later as well as wolfing the harmless olives, which by this time have taken on obscene and nauseating connotations.

Giovanni's foolishness – a corollary of his political naïveté – is brought out further in his arguments both with Luigi and with the Sergeant. The topsy-turvy situation whereby the Communist worker is the upholder of law and order and the policeman the subversive is an irony Fo relishes and expands further in the play. It is necessary, he is arguing, to question and to challenge, not to accept the *status quo* as Giovanni so obediently does. Hence the Sergeant can rightly state, 'You working classes have got to stop seeing us police as ignorant twits', whilst Giovanni is left to exclaim, 'Well, fuck a brick! . . . Whatever next. The died-in-the-wool, raving, steeped-in-Marxism, out-and-out red copper! Right in there with the lunatic fascists, psycho bullies and subnormal everyday street coppers' (Ibid., p. 12).

True to the conventions of farce, things are seldom what they seem. Fo takes this further with the added comic device of having the actor who plays the Sergeant reappear in a variety of disguises. Most significantly, his next appearance is as the officious Inspector, who precisely bears out the truth of all Giovanni's prejudices.

There is throughout the play a biting contrast between these two characters, the former a *poliziotto*, the latter a *carabiniere*. There is no British equivalent for the distinction between the two forces, and it is therefore difficult for a British audience to grasp the point of Fo's satire here. The police (*polizia*) have more power and authority, being better educated. A degree (for what that is worth in Italy) is obligatory for higher office. The *carabinieri*, on the other hand, perform the more unimportant jobs and are recruited from the vast potential labour force. They are the butt of endless Italian jokes owing to their lack of education and the fact that the vast majority of *carabinieri* in the North are emigrant workers from the underdeveloped South. Fo exaggerates the qualities of the two policemen to extremes, so that the Sergeant is ludicrously overeducated, a victim of his own reading, and the Inspector is even more gullible than Giovanni, notably in his swallowing of Antonia's story about Saint Evlalia. Behind this satiric presentation is another, more fundamental economic and political reality: that the intelligent man is being driven through unemployment into a profession he despises; and that the unthinking policeman is an ally of the bosses in their oppression of the worker. The savagery of the latter irony emerges in the original when the police are seen (and heard) to be active agents in the suppression of justice, a vital aspect of the *dénouement* which is altered in the British version.

It is when Giovanni and Luigi are surprised by the Police Sergeant as they find the sacks which have fallen from an overturned lorry that Fo's comedy most fully combines the serious and the comic. Here the economic

issue explored elsewhere in the context of the home and
day-to-day realities of making ends meet is expanded into
a condemnation of the international situation. The sacks,
which appear to contain caustic soda, are in fact full of
sugar, flour and rice. The deception is part of a large-scale
exploitation of flaws within the Common Market system
to inflate food prices so as to benefit unscrupulous
industrialists. It is precisely this type of manipulation of
the economy with the connivance of the legislature which
creates the shortages and high costs which have driven
the women to take the law into their own hands. The
explanation of this is all the more effective coming as it
does from the Sergeant, who tells Giovanni and Luigi,

> Do you know what will happen from here? I shall write
> a full report, a model of brevity and procedure, as the
> result of which charges will be laid. A brief item on
> News at Ten will allude to a brilliant police operation
> where contraband has been seized and men are sought.
> Duly alerted by the said item the industrialists will take
> a quick fortuitous trip over the border. Having laid my
> evidence before the judge, he will, with a pained
> expression, because it's a bit like welching on your own
> kind, sentence them to four months. The industrialists
> will hear about this whilst sunning themselves on the
> beaches of St Tropez and will immediately appeal to
> the President who will commute the sentence to a stiff
> fine. (*Can't Pay? Won't Pay!*, p. 30)

Partly as a result of the policeman's arguments, but more
particularly because Luigi informs him he's been made
redundant – a piece of information he has so far been
unable to impart because of the relentless pace of the
action – Giovanni turns thief and, along with Luigi, steals

59

some of the contraband food. The speed of the play increases still further and the plot becomes even more convoluted as Antonia, surprised by the Inspector with a large bag of vegetables under her coat, is driven to inspired invention in her tale of Saint Evlalia. The saint's festival, she says is being observed by all the women in the area, who carry food on their stomachs to honour her miraculous pregnancy in advanced years. Heedless of the curse that may fall on him, the Inspector disbelieves, but, when the lights suddenly go out (the electricity bill along with all the others has not been paid), he thinks he has been stricken with blindness. This is just the first of a series of comic humiliations that are piled on him.

All is ready for the play's *dénouement*, in which the arrival of Antonia's father (the final role of the actor who impersonates both policeman, and an undertaker) brings both the women and the men to the point where they are forced to admit stealing. This final scene reveals as consummate a skill in combining farce with serious political satire as the *dénouement* of *Anarchist*, but yet again the British adaptation opts for a more straightforwardly comic solution. Giovanni's analysis of the situation, his determination to fight in the face of the bloody police action which is taking place offstage, and the final affirmation of solidarity – first in a lyrical speech by Giovanni and then in a choric expansion of this taken up by the entire cast – counterpoint the farcical twists of the drama's unravelling. This produces a theatrical effect which is much more complex and challenging than that of the British adaptation, which works out its resolution through a series of personal reconciliations rather than through a confrontation of the problems faced by the individual in his dealings with society.

## 'Trumpets and Raspberries'

The third of Fo's popular farces is – from the point of view of its genesis and subject-matter – the most serious of all. A play about the kidnapping of Gianni Agnelli, the head of the Fiat corporation and one of the most powerful men in Italy, was a daring theatrical project. With Fo impersonating 'L'Avvocato' himself there was a more serious satiric potential than in his earlier drama *Il Fanfani rapito* (1975), which casts the diminutive Christian Democrat leader as a kidnap victim. It transpires that the kidnap is the work of Fanfani's own party, who were finding him an electoral liability. Fanfani had long been a figure of fun, not only in Fo's drama; Agnelli was an altogether more serious subject for satire.

It is revealing to note that Fo's original intention had been to write a play about the kidnapping and murder of Aldo Moro in 1978, a dramatisation of real events and – moreover – a tragedy. In a lengthy interview with Roberto Sciubba in *Avanti* in May 1979, Fo outlined his plans for this work, which would conclude with 'the symbolic act of the stripping of Moro, the denial, slowly at first, then more savage, of any form of public personal credibility. The drama comes to its climax with this act which immediately precedes his murder: as in a Greek tragedy.' As Fo outlines the tragic element in Moro's downfall the parallel with another drama – *King Lear* – is even more marked:

I believe the high point of his tragedy is when from being a man of power who is unable to comprehend the nature of power because he's inside the system, he seems, once he's outside it to understand the monstrosity of the power he once was a part of and for which he was once responsible. And what emerges is a transformation, bit by bit, letter by letter, of someone who instead of being powerful turns into an ordinary man, stripped of all privilege, all rank, all roles, of all that apparatus that gives him the luxury of another language.

Fo finished only the first act of this drama – complete with satyrs, narrator and chorus of Christian Democrats – before abandoning the project. The core of the work – and most notably the element of tragic *catharsis* resulting from *peripeteia* (reversal) and *anagnorisis* (realisation), as outlined above – found its way into the very different play about Agnelli, though transformed into the more familiar satiric *dénouement* characteristic of the farceur Fo.

Unfortunately it was precisely this element which was cut in the British adaptation. *Trumpets and Raspberries* is overall very much closer to the original than either of the other two adaptations we have discussed (and for this reason is more properly discussed solely within the scope of this chapter). It does, however, excise a fair amount of serious political discussion towards the end of the play and thus – like the adaptations of *Anarchist* and *Can't Pay? Won't Pay!* – opts for a simpler and less challenging *dénouement*. By the time the play reached the West End, almost all of the references to Moro had disappeared from the play and, for the benefit of British audiences, it was felt expedient to explain – in the form of a witty and ingenious aside within an aside – the role and significance of Agnelli in Italian society. Describing him as a sort of cross between the Duke of Kent and John DeLorean, and explaining that the inadvertent saving of Agnelli's life by the Fiat worker Antonio might be likened to a rescue of Coal Board chairman Ian McGregor by miners' leader

Arthur Scargill (opponents in a long and bitter miners' strike), the adaptation cleverly provided British analogies for Italian realities without detracting unduly from the Italian setting of the action. The awkward mixture of locations as essentially Italian political circumstances are shifted to a British or American setting is a feature which weakens the British adaptation of *Can't Pay? Won't Pay!* and makes complete nonsense of the American adaptation of *Anarchist*.

Unfortunately, however, the British ignorance of Italian politics renders *Trumpets and Raspberries* innocuous, even meaningless. The play works very well as a farce with political overtones, but the integration of the serious and the comic is inevitably lost. In London it was partly the nature of the West End audience and theatre circuit that was to blame, since the printed text of the British version at least remains faithful to Fo's original and discovers an altogether more satisfactory dramatic style than the two other adaptations, mediating with considerable skill between British and Italian vernacular styles. For example, when Antonio describes how the terrorists took pot shots at him – 'e anche loro giù a spararmi come fossimo al Luna Park' ('and they all started shooting at me as though we were in a fairground' – *Clacson, trombette e pernacchie*, 1981, p. 11) – we have 'Bang bang.' It was like Starsky and Hutch. Like Sam Peckinpah come back to life, and it wasn't in slow motion either' (*Trumpets and Raspberries*, 1984, p. 7). The translation cleverly solves the crucial difficulty of Agnelli's addressing Rosa with the polite pronoun 'lei' by having him address her as 'Madam' throughout – a device which gave an immense amount of comic opportunity to Griff Rhys Jones. And the translation scores brilliantly when, for example, it renders 'Faccia finta di essere Rognoni quanda fa la sua relazione alla

Camera: s'inventi tutti' ('Pretend to be Rognoni when he gives his speech to the House: make it all up' – *Clacson*, p. 81) – the Double's cue to Rosa before she launches on her 'confession' in the final scene – as 'Pretend you're a journalist from *The Sun*. Be inventive – make it all up!' (*Trumpets*, p. 60).

The comic structure of the play, however, was a feature appreciated by British critics. More so, it seems, than by those in Italy. Fo complained in *La stampa* that the Italian critics – with the notable exception of Luigi Lunari (a friend and admirer of Giorgio Strehler and an expert on Italian and Elizabethan theatre) – had entirely missed the point:

> I wrote this comedy with the theatrical machines of the sixteenth century in mind and with the typical characters of that period. Agnelli is in fact the Magnifico of the sixteenth century, the prototype of the modern capitalist whom Brentano talks about, who buys everything, from ships to nations. The worker is a scoundrel who has a wife and a mistress, also a classic character from the farces of the sixteenth century. There's even the mad doctor, straight out of the *commedia dell'arte*. If the literary critic can't see this, then he's blind.
>
> (*La stampa*, 18 Mar 1981)

In another interview, in *Il messaggero*, Fo analysed more clearly how the comedy works. 'We are trying to see everything that goes on onstage in the light of the comic and the grotesque. Mockery, a sense of humour related to facts and real people, destroys terror', he argued, continuing,

Within *Clacson, trombette e pernacchie* there is a geometric pattern, a deployment of characters and situations which derives from the Greek and Roman farces – from Plautus and Terence. In the futile search for originality you risk destroying systematically any real warm understanding of how people behave and feel, both onstage and off.

(*Il messaggero*, 15 Jan 1981)

The 'geometric pattern' is observable in the clever co-ordination of the exits and entrances of the central actor playing the double role of Antonio and Agnelli, a technique which owes something, perhaps, to Plautus (*The Menaechmi* in particular), but even more to Fo's own experience perfected over the years and traceable back to his second full-length play, *Aveva due pistole con gli occhi bianchi e neri*, in which he impersonated both a priest suffering from amnesia and a gangster on the run. In this play he invented a stage trick which he was able to put to good use in *Trumpets and Raspberries*: that of recording his character's final exit lines on tape so that he could go offstage earlier and so have extra time to prepare for his next entrance, at another point on the set, as the other character. The farcical crafting is more clearly observable in his employment of stage machinery. In the first scene immense comedy is extracted from the apparatus in the hospital. Here again we observe Fo's technique of using visual stage props to emphasise a serious point. For example, when Rosa has made her very pointed criticism of Luisa, one which strikes a satirical chord which has reverbations well beyond the personal issues dramatised in the play –

> Of course she was always there behind him . . . the
> bitch, egging him on. Because she's an extremist. She
> doesn't even have a Party card . . . Nothing! Not even
> a Socialist Party card! She's one of those intellectuals
> who are always trying to teach us, the working class,
> everything. The kind of people who are crazy about the
> masses, but can't stand crowds!   (*Trumpets*, p. 3)

– she grabs hold of one of the strings supporting the body
on the bed, with the result that pandemonium is created.

In Act II, Fo extracts every ounce of comic potential
from the assembly and operation of the monstrous machine
designed to feed patients through the nose. The doubting
of Antonio and Agnelli means that, when Agnelli explains
to Rosa that he has to be strapped down to be fed, we
anticipate, in the best traditions of farce, that the unwilling
Antonio will be the victim. This is what happens, and to
silence Antonio's protests Rosa puts his clarinet in his
mouth:

> *She takes the serviette out of his mouth, and inserts the
> clarinet's mouthpiece.* ANTONIO *moves the fingers of his
> right hand up and down the keys of the clarinet, which
> gives out a blues sequence of high and low notes,
> commenting grotesquely on the situation.*

Shortly afterwards,

> ROSA *takes some pieces of meat and puts them into the
> meat-grinder. The clarinet's wailing transforms into a
> desperate rock rhythm.* ROSA, *unperturbed, continues
> grinding, turning the handle of the mincer.* (Ibid.,
> pp. 49–50)

When the police arrive it is not long before they realise the usefulness of the machine as a torture device for extracting confessions from suspects. Since Antonio does not tell them what they want to know, the Inspector instructs his subordinate, 'Give the handle a little twirl.' When Antonio shouts, 'I'll tell all . . . I'll spill the beans . . . just set me free', the Inspector remarks, 'What a wonderful little machine.' We ought to have a little gadget like that down at the nick!' (ibid., p. 51). The comedy takes on a decidedly darker tone as the piece of farcical apparatus becomes a pointer to the whole issue of the state's attitude to terrorism.

The structure of the farce enables Fo to comment on several of the key issues which were preoccupying Italy at the end of the 1970s. They are issues which it is very difficult for a British – still less an American – audience to appreciate fully. The irony of the play is that, whilst it deals with the subject of terrorism, the reality is never presented in the work. Agnelli has not in fact been kidnapped; Antonio is not an agent of the Red Brigades; Rosa is not the organiser of a terrorist cell. The situation is quite different from that in either of the two other farces we have discussed: in both of these the realities of the situation that supplies the theme (in *Anarchist*, police misconduct and the distortion of evidence; in *Can't Pay? Won't Pay!*, the methods of coping with the most basic of economic needs, hunger) are tangibly presented on stage. It is unfortunate that, of these three farces adapted for the British stage, *Trumpets and Raspberries*, the most faithful to the original, proved in performance to be the most straightforwardly comic, the most completely diverting.

This is because the sheer ingenuity, the striking brio, of Fo's comic devices in the work tends to mask the seriousness of the satire for non-Italian audiences. Take the end of Act I, when Agnelli – whom the police assume to be Antonio – is interrogated in hospital. The irony is cleverly judged and the British adaptation rises superbly to the challenge, notably in its version of the gag when Agnelli/Antonio, recalling his childhood, tells the police that he used to own the football team Juventus, but got bored with it and gave it to his brother: this becomes 'I remember when I was fourteen I was given a cowboy outfit . . . and I've been running it ever since' (*Trumpets*, p. 21). This type of satire works very well; but it is when Agnelli/Antonio begins to talk about terrorist activities that it becomes impossible to re-create for non-Italians the impact of Fo's original on his own countrymen. The joke is that the police think a worker, a member of the Red Brigades, has turned supergrass, whereas the audience know he is Agnelli. Therefore any detail which appears to confirm the police – and media – presupposition that terrorism is essentially a leftish plot in fact indicates that behind the majority of terrorist activities is a bigger conspiracy between generals, judges and ministers. Therefore, when Antonio/Agnelli, who appears to know far too much, threatens to give details, the examining magistrate is determined to keep him quiet and has him repeatedly sedated. Fo has here set up a theatrical device guaranteed to have an Italian audience on the edge of their seats, expectantly waiting to see if the actor/dramatist will take advantage of this invention to speak out openly and similarly name names.

But Fo has another – more serious – aim, which emerges at the end of the play. This is to reveal the great and essential difference between the positions of Moro and Agnelli as men of power. The British version retains the visual joke, a Brechtian *gestus* of great force which found its way into the later performances of Fo's play. This is when the Inspector climbs up the pile of furniture to Agnelli and reaches out to touch his outstretched hand in a *'grotesque allusion to Michelangelo's famous "Creation" painting in the Sistine Chapel'*. As Agnelli comments, 'I created you. Go forth', pointed emphasis is given to his previous comments:

> Tell me, have you never read Karl Marx? Ah yes, of course. . . . These days only we captains of industry study *Das Kapital*. . . . Especially where it says: 'The only true power is financial–economic power, in other words, holding companies, markets, banks, commodities, in other words, Capital.' (*Trumpets*, p. 67)

The point is that Moro was sacrificed – as a mere politician – 'to save the respectability of the aforementioned financial state, not for the supporting services for which nobody gives a damn'.

In a three-page speech cut from the British version, Agnelli explains his reason for not giving himself up to the police: he knows that, like earlier crises, the kidnap will save the government from passing reforms, or, worse still, from being overthrown. He discusses how the Christian Democrats were saved from a petroleum scandal by the panic and concern conveniently created by an earthquake in Southern Italy, and then how the determination of the Communist Party to form a more radical opposition to the government was scotched by the kidnapping of the magistrate d'Urso (a burning issue in early 1981 when the play was premiered). A British audience might well appreciate the parallel between such developments and Mrs Thatcher's exploitation of the

Falklands invasion to distract attention from economic problems at home, but they would be unlikely to comprehend the finer details of recent Italian history.

Nor would Fo's indignation at the way his fellow politicians so callously treated Moro be very meaningful in a foreign context. With regard to his original project, Fo comments in his interview with Sciubba,

> I have taken Moro's correspondence and have made it into a running dialogue. There are facts – separate historical details – which when put together amount to a violence which is often obscene. For instance the wisecrack of Scalfari: he's just a puppet; we can't be expected to deal with a puppet in the hands of the Red Brigades. (*Avanti*, May 1979)

Much more material from Moro's letters found its way into the original version of *Trumpets and Raspberries* than is present in the British adaptation, most notably a well-known reflection of the kidnapped man:

> Dear friends, it has to be admitted that the experience I'm undergoing as a prisoner, though tragic, has helped me to understand a number of things. When you are inside power you are without eyes. Power is like a great Oedipus who single-handedly tears out his eyes so as not to see the truth. (*Clacson*, p. 75)

Such quotations, put into the mouth of Agnelli, immensely strengthen the seriousness and depth of political analysis in the work.

In like manner, the play's farcical devices draw attention throughout to the serious theme and situation which originally inspired it. In the last scene Fo invents a whole pantomime of moving furniture in which each item contains a hidden agent. This effectively communicates – albeit through a farcical distorting glass – the confusion created by the rivalry of sections of the Italian secret police with the anti-terrorist squad, and the paranoia of a state obsessed with the reality of terrorism. When the agents dismantle the bugging apparatus which has been put there previously, the Group Leader radios to base, 'I've located the hidden microphones. Must be the f. . .ing anti-terrorist mob. . . . Yes already dealt with.' In the original the reference is more precise: the Group Leader refers to 'classico lavoro di quelli di dalla Chiesa' – the typical operation of the anti-terrorist police under the orders of General dalla Chiesa. The play refers to the General throughout: during this period the ethics of his tactics in encouraging terrorists to 'grass' on their comrades were hotly debated. When Rosa makes her false confession – a magnificent parody of the worst suspicions and most hare-brained theories of terrorism – she insists at first on speaking to Mister Big, dalla Chiesa, in person (dalla Chiesa himself arrives in the cinema where she has her rendezvous with an agent, a priest in drag).

There is more than a little irony here. Franca Rame herself is involved in both Amnesty International and Soccorso Rosso, the organisation founded to help political prisoners in Italy. When the play was premiered in Milan, Rame and Fo brought onstage after the performance three women relatives of political prisoners incarcerated at Trani, one of whom read out a denunciation of conditions in the prison there. This incident triggered off bitter recriminations in both the right-wing and the left-wing press. Fo and Rame were accused of being supporters of the Red Brigades, though their continued criticism of terrorism is well known. The events of the previous year, when on grounds of their supposed sympathy for terrorism they were denied a visa to enter the United States, were repeating themselves. The British version makes no mention of dalla Chiesa, perhaps because he would mean little to a British audience, but more probably because by the time *Trumpets and Raspberries* was premiered in Britain the General was dead. In 1982, after his successful campaign to stamp out terrorism in Italy he decided to take on the Mafia. After setting in motion a plan for the comprehensive exposure of Mafia activities he flew down to Palermo, where he and his young wife were gunned down in the main street, Via Roma. Even more than Aldo Moro, dalla Chiesa was a tragic victim of his own hubris, the belief that he was indispensable and could do anything. It was he who, in the image of the blind and arrogant Oedipus determined to cleanse Thebes of the plague, more completely fitted the role of the tragic hero.

# 3
# Translation and Adaptation

Cose belle ne ho viste poche, alcune sono dignitose, altre sono dei massacri, sia per gli attori, sia per la regia, sia per il testo in genere corretto ma spesso svilito. Si tende sempre ad esaggerare, si recita il vaudeville o la commedia all'americana, ma questo fa parte della non comprensione nei riguardi della commedia dell'arte. Non sanno i tempi, non hanno misura, 'recitano' sempre un po' troppo, sbracano, come si dice in teatro.

[I've seen very few adaptations that have impressed me; some were worthy attempts, others travesties, whether on account of the actors, the direction or the text – accurate enough overall, but invariably in effect debased. There's always a tendency to exaggerate, to perform in the manner of music hall or vaudeville – a mistake which derives from the lack of understanding of the commedia dell'arte tradition. These performers lack a sense of timing, of genuine pace; there's always

an element of overacting, of laying it on with a trowel,
let us say.]

(Fo, in *Sipario*, Aug–Sep 1985)

In the previous chapters I have hinted at the complex –
and often confusing process – which characterises the
passage of a Dario Fo text from its original theatrical
representation in Italy to its performance in Britain.
As we have seen, the definition of what consitutes the
performance text of a Fo work is not easy to define, as
even the playscript itself is subject to a great deal of
modification both in rehearsal and during performance.
In this chapter we shall be concerned with the further
modifications which have occurred in the process of
translating that text into English.

If we glance at the four Fo texts published in English we
straightaway encounter a significant feature: the distinction
between the 'translator' and the 'adapter'. This situation
is basic to the manner by which Fo's plays have reached
British audiences, and is responsible for one of the most
fundamental problems of performance: the distortion of
his ideas in the passage from one language (and culture)
to another. All translation is by its very nature a matter
of compromise. There is no such thing as a definitive
translation, as what might serve perfectly in one period is
rendered inadequate fifty, even twenty, years later. The
English translations of Pirandello undertaken on a large
scale either during his lifetime or in the late 1950s and
early 1960s present real problems for the modern actor.
Pirandello's rhetoric – with its constant repetition and
affinity with poetic speech – was easier to translate into
an idiom which found a complementary expression in the
poetic dramas of Eliot and Fry and the elegant bourgeois

comedies of Coward and Maugham. A more naturalistic colloquial idiom is fatal to his plays – either in the translation or in the performance; but a contemporary actor finds his explicit overstatement of philosophical issues very difficult to handle. The translator of Fo is faced with the problem of finding a style which remains true to the original while employing a living theatrical language which the contemporary British actor can handle.

This problem has not always been squarely faced. It is necessary, if any translation is not to be a mere one-sided travesty of the orignal, for the translator to have in mind throughout both the original text and the new audience for whom he is writing. This may seem obvious, but, if we take the definition of translation given by Susan Bassnett-McGuire in her important work *Translation Studies*, we can see that such a procedure has not always characterised the process of transmission of Fo's dramas from Italian into English:

> What is generally understood as translation involves the rendering of a source language (SL) text into the target language (TL) so as to ensure that (1) the surface meaning of the two will be approximately similar and (2) the structures of the SL will be preserved as closely as possible but not so closely that the TL structures will be seriously distorted. (*Translation Studies*, 1980, p 2)

The problem in Fo's case is that the translations made in Britain have – with one exception – been effected by a combination of translator and adapter: (at least) two individuals, the former in control of the source language, the latter of the target language. This means that, with no one person in a position to weight the values of both, a huge area of distortion is possible. In what is sadly becoming an accepted working method in the British theatre, a so-called 'literal' translation is commissioned and then passed on to a theatre practitioner (be it dramatist or actor) who makes this 'playable'. In the case of *Female Parts*, Margaret Kunzle and Stuart Hood were credited with the 'translation', which was then 'adapted' by a non-Italian-speaker, the playwright Olwyn Wymark. Whilst this may be considered in theatrical and political terms a professional solution, by more academic or literary standards it is thoroughly amateur. However – with the exception of Hood's version of the monologue *Medea*, which makes no attempt to capture the roughness of the original dialect and thus sacrifices its toughness and down-to-earth directness – this particular adaptation in fact succeeds in fulfilling the requirements of the definition quoted above whilst providing a sound and effective performance text.

This is probably because the person responsible for the adaptation was a playwright and not a performer. Something different takes place when the actor (or company) begins to interpret the play, a factor which complicates still further the translation process of a theatrical text. Every performance of *Female Parts* constitutes a different interpretation, each actress (and director) shifting the emphasis and each audience responding in a different way. But the potential for distortion here (as against genuine and creative interpretation) is far less than is the case when the playscript is more directly created by the performer or performers. There is a marked difference between the Pluto Press published edition of *Trumpets and Raspberries* (close to Fo's original) and the text performed by Griff Rhys Jones at the Watford Palace and the Phoenix theatres. Yet the differences here were attributable to the performer's need to improvise some elements: a speech (which quickly became a set piece) explaining the significance of Gianni Agnelli, and various asides and retorts directed at the audience, and changing from performance to performance. These interpolations were very much in the style of Fo himself and gave the play a freshness and vitality it would have lacked had there been no flexibility in the performance text.

The *Trumpets and Raspberries* script carries this credit: 'Translated and adapted by R. C. McAvoy and A. M. Giugni', a statement which hides the fact that translator and adapter were in fact one and the same person. Precisely because such a situation is regarded as suspect in the British theatre – the hand of a better-known practitioner being considered virtually obligatory at some stage of the translation process – he has preferred to preserve his anonymity behind these pseudonyms. It is, however, because only one person prepared this text that it is the most genuine translation of a Fo play into English.

The playing text of *Accidental Death of an Anarchist* is without doubt a greater achievement as a comic acting script. But its resemblance to Fo's original is far more shadowy. In the translation process major distortion has taken place – not only of Fo's plot and message, but also, inevitably, of his theatrical language. The play was 'translated' by Gillian Hanna but adapted by Gavin Richards in the production for Belt and Braces Roadshow Company; even more significantly, Richards' own performance as the Maniac when the play transferred to the West End brought further changes. On the most basic level the performance style of the piece is a far cry from that required by Fo, both in its visual humour and in its verbal language. This is far and away the most lively and witty adaptation of Fo in English, the result being in several ways closer to the comedy of Orton than to that of Fo himself. Take this exchange when the Maniac is forcing the police literally to re-enact the interrogation of the anarchist:

SUPERINTENDENT: It was more or less like this: the suspect, the anarchist was sittting here.

*Indicates his own chair.* MANIAC *gets* SUPERINTENDENT *up and sits in the chair.*

MANIAC I'll play the anarchist. Go on.

SUPERINTENDENT: My colleague . . .

MANIAC: Ah ah . . .

SUPERINTENDENT: I mean . . . I . . . entered.

MANIAC: Go on then.

SUPERINTENDENT: What?

MANIAC: Enter.

SUPERINTENDENT *exits and re-enters. Goes over to* MANIAC.

SUPERINTENDENT: 'It's no use trying to pull the wool over my eyes, sonny.'

MANIAC: That's not what I've got here. This is a documentary reconstruction. I want the exact words in the exact manner.

SUPERINTENDENT *re-exits and re-enters aggressively*

SUPERINTENDENT: 'Right you filthy pox-ridden pansy you piss me about one more time and I'll . . . !'

MANIAC: Sorry to interrupt. It was 'piss me about'?

SUPERINTENDENT: I think so.

MANIAC: Good. Carry on.

SUPERINTENDENT: 'We've got incontravertible proof you're the murdering turd who planted the bombs in the railway station.'

(*Accidental Death of an Anarchist*, pp. 13–14)

Here we see the process of adaptation which characterises the language of the British version. The highly colloquial expressions used by the Superintendent in the two (very different) versions of his initial remark to the accused are a far cry from the Italian originals. In Fo's text there is simply a quibble over whether the expression he used was *prendere in giro* or *prendere per il sedere*, both of which mean 'to pull someone's leg', the second being more down-to-earth as it literally means 'to take by the seat'. The joke is that the Superintendent never used the more forceful phrase *prendere per il culo, culo* being the word for 'arse'. This altercation has been elaborated into the far funnier English text, which, however, owes nothing to the language patterns of the original. The whole acting text has been adapted in this way: for example, the original Italian of the expression 'We've got incontravertible proof you're the murdering turd,' at the end of above passage, means simply 'We've got the proof you were the person'. Another subtle alteration makes for a very different effect in the translation. In Fo's script this interrogation scene is merely reported; it is not acted out. The sequence of stage directions as the Maniac plays the part of the anarchist and the Superintendent replays the scene to wildly comic effect may seem authentic enough, recalling, as it does, the technique of Pirandello in *Six Characters in Search of an Author*, but it is not found in Fo's original. Such metatheatrical effects – constantly reminding us that we are in a theatre through a burlesque of the idiom – are perhaps not very far removed from the comedy of Fo, but at times they seem to be indulged in too much for their own sake and threaten to distract us from the serious cut of the satire.

In passages such as the one quoted above, the process of adaptation is so complete and so successful that it would be perverse to insist on a 'betrayal' of the original. Yet it is important to realise just how very different in tone the two versions are before going on to examine the more significant alterations to the play's structure, since such an extensive alteration of Fo's theatrical syntax inevitably plays its part in what he has called the 'erosion at a satirical level' which affects 'the relationship of the tragic to the grotesque'. Again and again in the British adaptation we are reminded of the verbal dexterity of the comedy-of-manners genre in general and of the way it is used by a writer such as Orton in particular. Immediately after the passage cited above, the Maniac in Fo's original concludes,

> Of course, of course, it's self-evident. I'd say obvious. Just as it's undoubtedly the case that the bombs at the station were planted by a railway worker, we can also assert in consequence that the bombs at the Palace of Justice in Rome were planted by a judge, that those at the tomb of the Unknown Soldier were planted by the captain of the guard and the one at the Agricultural Bank was planted by a banker or a farmer, take your pick! (*Morte accidentale di un anarchio*, 1974, pp. 33–4)

In the British adaptation this is metamorphosed into:

> Of course, of course, it's self-evident. So as it was undoubtedly the case that a *railway worker* must have planted the bombs in the *railway station*, then we can also assert that the famous bombs in the law courts must have been planted by a lawyer, the one at the Agricultural Bank by a bank clerk or a cow, whichever takes your fancy, and the bomb at the tomb of the

Unknown Soldier undoubtedly perpetrated by a corpse. (*Anarchist,* p. 14)

Fo's exposé of the farcical logic of the police is the cue for more baroque effects in the translation, a relish of word-play which a few lines later transforms Fo's straightforward statement 'I'm here to conduct a serious inquiry, not to play around with stupid syllogisms' into the crackling retort 'I'm here to conduct a serious enquiry not fart about with syllogistic prattling.'

The British adaptation of *Anarchist* may employ a language far removed from that of the original, but it represents in its own right a playing script of immense vitality which exploits to the full the potential of both farce and of witty comedy of manners. In so doing it emphasises the fact that the British comic tradition is in many respects very different from the Italian. The sophistication and complexity of the linguistic idiom employed in the British version of *Anarchist* points to a theatrical heritage which goes back to the Restoration and encompasses representative figures from Wilde and Coward through to Pinter, Orton and Bond. Witty social satire has been a distinctive element of British comedy and has always been a powerful weapon in the fight against hypocrisy and social injustice.

This needs to be stated firmly since when we come to the British adaptation of *Can't Pay? Won't Pay!* we shall find ourselves up against a text which Tony Mitchell – loud in his denunciation of the *Anarchist* adaptation – has described as follows:

It remains the most accurate and plausible version of a Dario Fo play in the UK . . . the spirit of the original is

maintained, the relatively few cuts and alterations . . .
placing the play in an English working class context . . .
improve on the original. Walker transformed Fo's play
into a genuinely down-to-earth, working-class colloquial
idiom which fixed the play firmly in an appropriate
English context while maintaining the Italian names
and references essential to the play's plot and
situation   (*Dario Fo: People's Court Jester*, 1984, p. 96)

I shall show that this opinion is a gross misinterpretation
of the case, since the British version of *Can't Pay? Won't
Pay!* is in every way a more complex distortion than the
British *Anarchist*, being neither true to the original nor a
theatrical version with an integrity of its own.

In the first place, despite the involvement of *two*
adapters, the 'literal' translation – a nonsensical phrase,
since it implies some fidelity to the original independent
of sense in the target language and therefore, somehow,
a purely one-sided operation – is still painfully evident in
places. It is all too obvious that it was prepared by someone
whose native language is not English. Expressions such as
'rabbits me to death' (*Can't Pay? Won't Pay!*, 1982, p. 4),
'I haven't time to chit chat about drinking coffee all day'
(p. 4), 'very well nicked my dear' (p. 7) and 'appearances
can be deceiving' (p. 24) are ugly and awkward in the
extreme, and distort English idiom (for instance, in the last
example quoted the 'translator', Lino Pertile, presumably
means 'deceptive'). This clumsy text has then been taken
by Bill Colevill and given what Mitchell calls a 'working-
class colloquial idiom'. Presumably he has in mind such
outbursts as Giovanni's:

And goodnight! Well, fuck a brick! Lord love us.
Whatever next. The died-in-the-wool, raving, steeped-

in-Marxism, out-and-out red copper! Right in there with the lunatic fascists, psycho bullies and subnormal everyday street coppers. Well that's where the bleeding extremists fetch up, obviously. In the police! And he's got the neck to stand there in front of me, twenty years a member, and criticize the CP! From the left too! (*Can't Pay? Won't Pay!*, p. 12)

This is about as near a genuine working-class idiom as is the language of Wilde or Coward. It is certainly as patronising as Coward at his worst (in scenes from *Cavalcade*, for example), since it assumes that coarse expletives are enough to indicate that a character is working-class whilst ignoring the fact that the extreme sophistication of syntax and vocabulary employed here is a sign not so much of a working-class idiom as of bourgeois theatrical language posing as – and patronising – working-class speech. A glance at the plays of David Storey or D. H. Lawrence, or the opening scene of Bond's *Saved*, gives a truer idea of how working-class people speak: Colevill's invention represents the most superficial pastiche.

Bob Walker's adaptation using techniques from the world of music hall further complicates the issue. We shall see later how this affects characterisation and the mechanism of the farce; here it is sufficient to note that there is a total lack of correlation between character, situation and language. Whereas Gavin Richards in his *Anarchist* adaptation carefully observed the basic rule of comedy by making only his intelligent and cunning characters articulate (wit being a corollary of quick thinking and sharpness of mind), Bob Walker in *Can't Pay? Won't Pay!* shows himself blind to any such considerations throughout. The opening scene between Margherita and Antonia turns the whole conversation into a stand-up comic routine in which Margherita is the mere stooge, setting up Antonia's jokes. But these jokes are – significantly – on Antonia. The joky language – malapropisms, puns, word-play, extravagant references – from the start reveals the awkwardly mixed tone of the adaptation (and owes nothing to Fo). Quick repartee such as 'Competition. Can we enter?' (p. 2) and the references to *High Noon*, the storming of the Bastille and the Winter Palace are in flat contradiction to the malapropisms which characterise Antonia in other parts of this scene (e.g. 'murderer, pervert, paediatrician' or 'he copulated immediately'). The adapters simply cannot make up their mind whether Antonia is a dizzy cow or an astute and knowing freedom-fighter. In Franca Rame's performance there is, of course, nothing of the former about her. The resort to cheap theatrical tricks not only produces inconsistency in the character's language, but also thereby seriously undermines the politics of the play from the start.

**'Accidental Death of an Anarchist'**

We now move beyond the shift of language patterns to the more marked changes the adaptations effect in the theatrical structure of the dramas. It will be observed from the example quoted above (pp. 80–1) of how the Maniac ridicules the logic of the police inquiry that linguistic shifts almost imperceptibly affect the comic structure of the play. Moreover, the increased sophistication of the Maniac's language in the adaptation, as against Fo's original play, makes him a different character and edges the play consistently towards an accelerating zaniness of farcical improvisation. We have also observed how the persistent exploitation of the theatrical medium and the shattering of the fourth-wall convention of naturalistic comedy takes a basic feature of Fo's theatrical skill to greater extremes. The Maniac relishes his disguises far more in the British adaptation: not merely the initial impersonation of the Judge, but also his final metamorphosis into the forensic expert, a cross between Sherlock Holmes and Long John Silver. This is not in fact the final card in Fo's original play: the character's last appearance is as a cardinal complete with regalia and revolver. There is consequently rather more restraint in his previous impersonations. Fo's original audience were never allowed to lose sight of the serious and pressing contemporary political issue. Through the extremes of the farcical convolutions in the adaptation there is a real danger of this.

An example of the added element of comedy in the adaptation, and of its potential for distracting attention from the seriousness of the issues, is the treatment of a single speech by the Superintendent, which in the original runs,

> I've just had a phone-call from Rome . . . there's an interesting piece of news for you: your friend, sorry, colleague, the ballet-dancer has confessed . . . he's admitted he was the one who planted the bomb at the bank in Milan.
>
> (*Morte accidentale di un anarchio*, 1974, p. 35)

In the adaptation – aside from the fact that it is very difficult to take seriously the fact that Pinelli's 'colleague', Valpreda, was a ballet-dancer (a detail well known to the Italian audience) – there is a vast comic elaboration of this incident which begins with Pissani (again) re-enacting the scene: first offstage, where he practises 'I've just had a phone call from ROME!', 'I've just HAD a phone call from Rome!', 'I'VE just had a phone call from Rome!', only to re-enter and, predictably, announce, 'I've just had a rome call from Phone!' (*Accidental Death of an Anarchist,* 1980, p. 15). Further humour is extracted at the expense of Valpreda through the Maniac's additions 'This is the friend, the vaudeville dancer from the anarchist group in Rome. . . . The one that strings glass beads together. . . . Did he actually dance in the beads?' with his comment to the audience (so specified in the stage directions) 'Hilarious, isn't it?' This wasn't quite so unambiguously funny to Fo and his original audience, and an indication of the degree to which the British adaptation has loosened its hold on the serious satiric base of the play comes with the curious error 'your friend has confessed to planting the bomb in the Milan bank in Rome' (p. 16) – a mistake which is repeated a few lines later.

The British adaptation interrupts the Maniac's frightening of the police (by telling them that they are to be made examples of) with the discussion of the 'rewriting of events'. In the original this occurs *after* the terrorising episode and after Pissani has tried to throw himself out of the window. The Maniac's real motive for initiating the discussion is consequently blunted: in the original he rounds on the police and, after confessing it was all a trick, says, 'It's just one of the customary ploys or tricks the magistrature itself resorts to now and again to make the police realize how uncivil, not to say criminal, their methods can be' (p. 43). The biting irony is lost, as is the more serious parody of police methods when the two policemen refuse to go to the window and are dragged there by the Maniac. Pissani's comic remorse in the British version – 'Famiglia, pardona me!' – is, in its (deliberately inaccurate) mock Italian, a farcical distraction. The British version significantly omits a further disturbing detail. The Maniac in his terrorising of the police cites an 'English' maxim: 'The boss lets his mastiffs loose on the peasants. If the peasants complain to the king, the boss, to get off the hook, kills the mastiffs.' This has a grim relevance for the police here, but the irony becomes still grimmer – in what is a very far cry from the tone of the adaptation – when the Maniac later admits it was all an invention, including the reference to the mastiffs, adding, 'No boss ever killed his dogs to give a peasant satisfaction. And if the dog dies in the struggle, the king sends a telegram of sympathy to the boss' (p. 43).

The Maniac's account of the noises emanating from the nearby police station (pp. 24–5) has a very different emphasis in the original. Again serious satire gives way in the adaptation to more farcical comedy. This is a true story: the audience would recognise the reference to Bergamo as surely as a British audience in the early 1960s had only to hear Sheffield mentioned on *That Was the Week that Was* to pick up the allusion to a notorious example of police brutality. In the adaptation, the Maniac begins by saying, 'I was holidaying in Bergamo a couple of summers back', which immediately gives the narrative an air of the improbable and the humorous, reinforced by the ironic detail after he announces that even the priest was arrested: 'in nomine spiritu sancti, you're nicked'. The British version characteristically starts to exaggerate at 'screams of merriment and mirth accompanied by thigh-slapping convulsions of humorous hysteria', the relish of word-play being evident in the alliteration, whilst the whole of the conclusion is elaborated from the cry 'Ha, stop it! Ha ha! No! Please! Mercy! I can't take any more!!' During this the actor *thrashes about laughing and miming being beaten'*, and he *'mimes broken nose and cauliflower ear*' as he talks of the 'wackey witty carabinieri . . . sending their suspects spinning across the floor in fits of fun', once again relishing the alliteration. In the television version by Belt and Braces this passage was expanded into new flights of comedy. Even the final comment has a particularly risible English emphasis in phrases such as 'a fucking good laugh' and 'in his grave right now, pissing himself', which are a far cry from the original. Fo's scene ends more soberly:

> SUPERINTENDENT: Leaving aside the irony, you know perfectly well that right from the chief constable down to the last copper they were all condemned, weren't they?
>
> MANIAC: Sure. For an over-developed sense of comedy! *The police pull faces to show their irritation.*
>
> (*Morte accidentale*, p. 58)

The point at which farce escalates into a more zany area is more firmly controlled by Fo. The change occurs in the discussion over galoshes, in the original a part of the Maniac's game, but in the British version a desperate invention on the part of Pissani. Thus the Superintendent's annoyance in the original when the Maniac casually suggests that the anarchist might have been a triped – a joke brushed quickly aside – is taken to much greater comic lengths in the adaptation:

> MANIAC: There's one little detail doesn't quite fit here. (*Looking at papers.*) Was the suspect triped, Superintendent?
>
> SUPERINTENDENT: (*relief turning to boiling rage*): I beg your pardon.
>
> MANIAC: This suicidal railwayman. If, by chance the

bugger's got three feet we're home and dry.
(SUPERINTENDENT nearly explodes.)
Temper! Temper! It'll end in tears.   (*Anarchist*, p. 26)

A particularly choice illustration of the sort of verbal sophistication indulged in by the adaptation but lacking in the original is provided by the description of the victim: Fo's 'the anarchist laid out on the edge of the courtyard had both his shoes still on his feet' becomes in the British version 'the jam sponge was accoutred with a pair of shoes consistent with the average biped'. And again the combination of the irresistible urge to play with words plus the vibrancy of its sexual slang inevitably makes the British adaptation more lively than the Italian original in the passage which follows, where Fo's

SUPERINTENDENT: But no, it's impossible! An anarchist with galoshes . . . that's something old fashioned, conservative . . .
MANIAC: Anarchists *are* very conservative.
(*Morte accidentale*, p. 67)

is turned into

SUPERINTENDENT: Galoshes are a ridiculous garment. An anarchist wouldn't be seen dead in them.
CONSTABLE: Exactly!
SUPERINTENDENT: Bloody balls, Constable!
CONSTABLE: Only trying to help.
SUPERINTENDENT: Cock! Complete cock!
(*Anarchist*, p. 27)

The corollary of this comic exuberance, however, is that the police are directly incriminated by the exchanges which follow, a conversation which the Maniac records and uses against them later. This is entirely invented in the adaptation and substitutes for the more subtle political satire of the original a device which is crudely comic.

The 'erosion at a satirical level' to which Fo refers in his discussion of adaptations which find 'solutions which are exclusively comic' is most clearly seen in the final part of the play. In the previous chapter we examined how the lengthy discussions between the Maniac and Feletti which constitute the serious meat of the drama are deliberately offset by the comedy: we follow with delight the humiliations heaped on Bertozzo as the truth of the Maniac's identity gradually and inevitably dawns on him and the others desperately try to shut him up. This is significantly disturbed in the adaptation, because, whilst the comedy is extended and exaggerated, the serious matters are undermined. Fo's cunning was to have Bertozzo gradually silenced; in the British version his interruptions get noisier and noisier as he is involved in an ever-accelerating plethora of visual gags. The very different tone of the adaptation can be seen in the pace of the interruptions: '*They launch themselves at* BERTOZZO. *He falls to the ground. They all end up on the ground. They chase him off through the door*' – a cops-and-robbers sequence which constantly interrupts, and upstages, the discussion between the Maniac and Feletti. Though the stage directions read, 'While BERTOZZO, CONSTABLE, SUPERINTENDENT *and* PISSANI *are wrestling on the floor the* MANIAC *continues oblivious*', the audience is quite unable to follow the argument. Moreover, a considerable exaggeration of the comedy with the props coupled with the verbal gags which act as punchlines further detracts from the seriousness of the issues, as with the following:

MANIAC: *produces another hand. Elegant, manicured, with nails varnished. He screws it on.* FELETTI *throws hand over her shoulder in revulsion. It lands in filing cabinet as* CONSTABLE *is closing drawer. His fingers get mashed.*

CONSTABLE: AAAH!

SUPERINTENDENT: This woman is getting out of hand. (*Anarchist*, p. 36)

More important is the underplaying of the serious discussion, much of which – concerning the opposed theories of terrorism, the *autunno caldo* or 'hot autumn' of 1969 when striking workers and students formed a powerful alliance, and the threat of a strong paramilitary state – is cut in the adaptation. Furthermore, most of what remains is treated in such a way that its significance is effectively inverted. Feletti (based closely on the real-life Camilla Cederna) is the chief exponent of Fo's 'counter-information' in the final part of the play, but the crucial facts she relates emerge less as details of this *controinformazione* than as incredible, ludicrous inventions. Her statement

Listen!! There have been 173 dynamite attacks in the last fourteen months, that's twelve a month, one every three days! It has been proved that 102 of these were the work of known fascists! There are serious indications that of the remaining 71 over a half are attributable to fascists or extreme right para-military groups!

(*Anarchist*, p. 37)

though an almost exact translation of the original, takes on a totally different meaning because of the stage direction which prefaces it: '*clinging desperately to her*

91

*performance*', which has no authority in Fo's drama. These are hard facts culled through research, not the ravings of a woman out of control. There is a significant undermining of the position of the women characters in several of the British adaptations, and that of *Anarchist* does not help by having the actress playing Feletti criticise Fo for creating only one female role. Even the punctuation of the above speech is indicative of the changed emphasis. The exclamation marks (double at the beginning) are a sure sign of the character's lack of control, which is carried over into the Maniac's exclamations when he attacks the system:

Expose the links between fascist politicians like those in the *M. S. I.*! and government ministers? Even turn the spotlight on *senior officers in the police force itself*?!! (Ibid.)

In their intemperate character these outbursts – aided and abetted by the indiscriminate satire of the adaptation, reaching its climax in the direction '*Gives detailed examples of political murder and state repression in Britain*' – are diametrically opposed to the very precise, carefully mounting argument of the original, which moves from analysis of specific issues and their consequences to a call for more radical political activity. Though the attack on the police force and the further implications of state complicity were powerful features of the original British production, this bite was soon lost in the transfer to the West End. Fo's Leninist viewpoint was never fully shared in Britain, his belief that

the magistrature and the police, whom the play places under accusation are not institutions to criticize or correct . . . they are the more direct expression of the bourgeois state, the class enemy which must be destroyed . . . we are convinced that we need a theatre which can describe the contemporary world to the people of today based on the understanding that it describes this world as one which can and must be changed.  (*Morte accidentale*, pp. 112–13)

Significantly too, Fo changed his original ending. The second version ends with the Maniac outmanoeuvring Bertozzo with the help of the bomb and leaving with the incriminating tape-recording which he says he will circulate to political parties, newspapers and ministers so that a real scandal can explode. A further farcical device had followed in the earlier version: there was a black-out, then an explosion offstage, and a cry for help from the Maniac. Feletti managed to escape and release the others. But a bearded individual then entered. His beard was 'real' and he announced himself as the 'real' judge (in a repetition of the trick employed previously in the comedy *Aveva due pistole con gli occhi bianchi e neri*). The investigation then continued. Fo thought this ending too neat and preferred instead the more provocative one whereby the incriminating evidence has an effect equivalent to that of his own drama. In opting for a two-way alternative *dénouement* the British adaptation departs most radically from the original. Skilfully and brilliantly as it reworks Fo's play for the British stage, in the end the adaptation is obliged to follow the implications of its inexorable movement away from its source to a radically different target.

### 'Can't Pay? Won't Pay!'

There is a fascinating irony in the opening of the British version of *Anarchist* when Bertozzo says,

> I ought to warn you that the author of this sick little play, Dario Fo, has the traditional irrational hatred of the police common to all narrow-minded left-wingers and so I shall, no doubt, be the unwilling butt of endless anti-authoritarian jibes.
>
> (*Accidental Death of an Anarchist*, 1980, p. 1)

In fact, of course, as Gavin Richards well knows, Fo's 'hatred' is not at all 'irrational'. His criticisms of the police – in *Anarchist* notably – are very precise. So is his analysis of the particular economic issues in *Can't Pay? Won't Pay!*, which – through the structure of the farce – carefully and precisely opens out to encompass the wider social issues. If the adaptation of *Anarchist* can be said to endanger the careful balance between farce and satire, the British version of *Can't Pay? Won't Pay!* bulldozes its way straight through the play and entirely destroys the dramatic structure, and with it any real potential for political satire.

Mitchell's dismissal of the *Anarchist* adaptation without any evaluation of its real (albeit highly original) strengths and his praise for the Walker version of *Can't Pay? Won't Pay!* as 'the most accurate and plausible version of a Dario Fo play in the UK' are, to put it kindly, very misleading. It would be more accurate to quote the Superintendent in *Anarchist*, who of the attempt to justify the rewriting of the facts tersely comments, 'Cock! Complete cock!' To date, no Fo play has been so totally – and wilfully – reworked for the British stage as *Can't Pay? Won't Pay!*

has; the commercial success of this adaptation in no way justifies its claim to represent the original accurately. When one discovers that the play has been successful in Israel (in itself an extraordinary irony in view of Fo's pro-Palestinian stand) it comes as no surprise to learn that the version performed there was not a Hebrew translation of Fo's original but a translation of the Walker adaptation! The word 'translation' begins to take on stratospheric implications which make it all the more important to examine precisely what Walker (and with him Pertile and Colvill) did with the original.

Let us look first at the presentation of the police in the original and in the adaptation. As we saw in Chapter 2, the essential running joke of the play revolves round the casting of the same actor as the Maoist *poliziotto* and the jobsworth *carabiniere*. It is a hard challenge to find an equivalent for this in English, and the adaptation makes no attempt to do so. Instead the two figures are brought much closer together, being presented in an equally ludicrous light. Take the stage business which accompanies the first entrance of the Sergeant, a sequence of gags wholly invented by Walker in the adaptation. (Indeed, this episode, along with many of the music-hall routines often felt to be so true to Fo's brand of popular humour, were added by Walker after the first production of the play at the Half Moon in 1978, and are not found in the earlier edition of the play published under the title *We Can't Pay? We Won't Pay!*)

SERGEANT *appears in window at rear, clinging to swaying drainpipe.*

SERGEANT: Oi. (GIOVANNI, *back to window, shoots arms up*.)

GIOVANNI: O my good God. I'll get shot in the back

resisting arrest. (SERGEANT *sways across window again.*)

SERGEANT: Oi!

GIOVANNI: All right, all right. I'll come quietly. (SERGEANT *sways back into view.*)

SERGEANT: Oi. You Desist. (*He hooks a foot over window-sill.*)

GIOVANNI: Desist? Desist? I am desisting, aren't I? What more can I desist?

SERGEANT: Does this flat belong to you?

GIOVANNI: Yes.

SERGEANT: I order you to assist me.

GIOVANNI: Oh, yeah? How? Beat myself up? Punch myself in the nuts?

SERGEANT: Help!

GIOVANNI: Stop mucking about.

SERGEANT: Help!

GIOVANNI: What a sense of humour. (*Now* GIOVANNI *turns round and sees policeman clinging to drainpipe with foot in saucepan on window-sill.*) I don't believe it. What are you playing at?

SERGEANT: Help! EEEEK!

(*Can't Pay? Won't Pay!*, 1982, pp. 9–10)

In Fo's original the policeman is presented seriously from the start, which makes his Maoist philosophy – when he begins to expound it – all the more amusing. It is significant that the best epithet Giovanni can think of in the British version is 'raving subversive' (p. 12); in the original he is carefully stigmatised as a 'Maoist'. The adaptation's excessive – and imprecise – jokiness in presentation of the police seriously undermines Fo's satire. The Italian police are not intrinsically funny or amiable. Italy is in some major respects (for a Western democracy) a frighteningly overpoliced state. This is in part due to unemployment, and the corollary ie that a veritable industry has developed for the provision of different types of police, private and public; the attractiveness of the profession is enhanced by the fact that, for many in Italy, the uniform confers the idea of rank, authority and prestige. The healthy contempt most people in Britain feel for anyone who wears a uniform is not shared by the Italians. Therefore, to present the police (whether it be the *polizia* or the *carabinieri*) on stage as ill-dressed idiots is grossly to misinterpret Fo's intention. It says something about the level of political education of Walker's – as against Fo's – audience that Walker feels the need to invent the whole business with the 'little red book' in order to underline the Sergeant's affinities with the far Left. But even this goes for very little given the sequence of visual and verbal gags introduced (in Walker's second version of the play) into this first scene with Giovanni and the Sergeant. Fo's complex political humour is replaced by this:

GIOVANNI: Know where you'll be tomorrow?

SERGEANT: No.

GIOVANNI: Beating me up on the picket line. That's where you'll be.

SERGEANT: You're so right. So terribly tragically right.

GIOVANNI: Too right, I'm right.

SERGEANT: But. But. Nevertheless. The police have stood back on occasions, you know. Even, dare I say, thrown themselves on the other.

GIOVANNI: Oh yeah, when?

SERGEANT: Venice Water Riots, August the 5th.

GIOVANNI: (*impressed*): Oh.

SERGEANT: 1723.

GIOVANNI:  Oh very relevant. Very topical. I won't hold
me breath till it happens again.
*(Can't Pay? Won't Pay!*, p. 12)

It seems very unfair that Fo should be saddled with this
nonsense, as his own version concludes with the Sergeant
saying, 'It might be that one of these days you'll learn that
the police have refused to go about beating people up for
the bosses . . . indeed, that they've thrown themselves in
with the other side' (*Non si paga, non si paga!*, 1974, p.
28).

A further – significant – alteration, which tells us a great
deal about the wit of the two versions, occurs in the
punchline to the story about the man who bought his dog
a hearing aid. Learning that the animal electrocuted itself
pissing, the Sergeant in the original – well aware the story
refers to him – retorts, 'Well, I'll make sure I never go
and cock my leg', (*Non si paga*, p. 62) which in the
adaptation becomes

*They laugh.* SERGEANT *looks puzzled.*
SERGEANT:  There's a moral to that story. Can't think
what.    (*Can't Pay? Won't Pay!*, p. 29)

Yet again one of Fo's clever double-edged political ironies
bites the dust.

It is also important to draw attention to the fact
that this type of distortion in the adaptation inevitably
encourages a further level of misinterpretation in the
performance. By the time we have completed the long
chain of interpreters which begins with the translator and
moves through the adapter, director and performer to the
audience we have often – as in this instance – reached a
point where the original is virtually unrecognisable. If the

translator's choice of language is careless, how much more effective is the destructive power of a misguided performance style in distorting the author's meaning! A large measure of responsibility for the destruction of the political potential of the play in the original West End production belongs to the actor Silvester McCoy – much praised for his portrayal of the combined roles of the policemen, old man and undertaker. It must be pointed out that the adaptation encourages a particular type of performance here, notably towards the end of the play, when the actor makes his appearance as undertaker, and the British version cannot resist adding a series of gratuitous music-hall jokes (again, found only in the later, revised version). But a more manic, over-the-top, self-indulgent piece of comic acting than that furnished by McCoy would be hard to imagine. This illustrates a danger to which British actors all too readily succumb in playing Fo: that of judging the performance solely by the number of laughs it obtains and thus allowing the farcical features to run away with the play rather than using them to score political points. Fo relishes the humour of assigning a large number of roles to the same actor (there are practical economic reasons for it too, of course). But the performer should not allow the required versatility to be the main – let alone the sole – inspiration for his performance. Otherwise there is a real risk of losing the thrust of Fo's satire, which combines the contrasted roles of *poliziotto* and *carabiniere*. Yet this is a point almost entirely lost in the adaptation, which omits Fo's most telling satirical stroke when Giovanni, reacting to the subversive Maoist Sergeant, comments, 'You see where the so-called "opposed extremisms" have ended up: in the police force!' (*Non si paga*, p. 28).

The strongest charge one can level against Walker's

adaptation is that it seriously diminishes the force of Fo's satire by relentlessly undermining the integrity of Giovanni's opponents. In the case of the police, this implies a minimising of the danger of the opposition; in the case of Antonia, the initial effect is a blunting of the irony, and the overall result an offensive distortion of the woman's role. Take for instance, the presentation of Antonia in her first scene with Giovanni. Crucial speeches by her are omitted: a technique which has the effect of weakening her character and intelligence. In the original she goads Giovanni, telling him the bosses think the workers are no better than dogs, and pours scorn on his lack of initiative:

> Stay put. I'll be back in no time. Just read your paper
> . . . or get over there and watch the telly; there's bound
> to be that wonderful Aldo Moro talking about the
> 'crisis', telling us it's serious but not desperate, that we
> should all pull together: rich and poor. Tighten our
> belts, be patient, understanding and have faith in the
> government and in *Canzonissima*. But before you begin
> to have faith in the government and in *Canzonissima*,
> I'll be back!   (*Non si paga*, pp. 21–2)

The references to Moro, the Christian Democrat Prime Minister referred to more significantly at the end of the play, and to *Canzonissima*, the television comedy programme for which Fo and Rame worked until their break with RAI in 1962 after their material had been censored and banned, are particularly difficult to translate for an English audience. (The lack of information on Moro seriously undermines *Trumpets and Raspberries*, yet it is interesting to observe that Fo can discuss the Profumo scandal with his Italian audience in *Anarchist*.) But it is just such on-the-ball criticism which makes Antonia more than a match for her husband.

The British adaptation relentlessly diminishes her, in such a way as to create a positively sexist substitute for the character presented (in both senses) by Franca Rame. When she shows the food to Giovanni the British stage direction reads, '*He sits at kitchen table. Antonia nervously selects a can at random and puts it in front of him.*' This is a stark travesty of the original, in which she '*bangs down two tins of dog food on the table.*' What are the adapters trying to do? Franca Rame is no timid, retiring little wife; no more is Antonia. Again, a little later, the adaptation invents a further stage direction: '*Antonia selects a packet at random and puts in front of him.*' Why '*at random*'? She knows – in the original, at any rate – precisely what she is doing. A subtler alteration in the presentation of Antonia occurs in the way the translation frequently has Antonia interrupt what are in the original long speeches by Giovanni. It might be argued that this is an effective method of representing the mocking aspect of the wife's role; but that is not how it emerges in performance. This apparently negligible alteration results in the reduction of her role to that of stooge: of stage fool.

There is later a much more serious – in some respects extraordinary – alteration of Fo which totally changes Antonia's status as woman and revolutionary. It is the description of the commune the women set up to sell their own biscuits when the factory decide to make them all redundant. (In fact – a small point, but one which explains an apparent anomaly in the translation – 'biscuits' is a very misleading translation; they were making *grissini*, (savoury bread sticks, which is why it was appropriate to be crying into the food – adding the salt!) Antonia's story is more convincing in the original because she cites specific facts:

the 'thousands of workers', for example, actually collected 80 million lire (about £40,000) – 'something that, if you hadn't been directly involved in, as I was, would take some believing'. More significantly, at the end of the story she comments, 'Questa, mica è una favola del buon cuore, e basta' – the equivalent of the English text's 'It's not just a fairy story, you know', but the sense is precisely the opposite: Antonia's tale is a true story (*Non si paga*, pp. 54–5). The way the British version deflates the whole enterprise by adding 'It ain't got a happy ending' and explaining how 'the C. P. [Communist Party] moved in' and ruined everything reveals the gap between Fo's political theatre and that of the British fringe. The deflating of the commune is perfectly typical of a trendily leftish British theatre group pouring scorn on what it considers the lunatic fringe. The fact that the adaptation makes the villains the Communist Party conceals a further irony. As one of the two major political parties in Italy, the Communist Party is regarded by progressive political thinkers there as representing a type of conservatism (not far removed from that of the SDP in Britain): hence the reactionary stand taken by the Communist Giovanni in the play. One has only to consider Franca Rame's own position – demonstrated by her spirited description in the *Arena* television interview in 1984 of how the company co-operated in the sale of 10,000 glasses before one of their performances in Bologna to raise money for redundant factory workers – to realise that the alteration of the commune story is the boldest travesty of Fo's message: a cheap pandering to bourgeois theatrical taste.

It is very difficult to understand how, if he had read – let alone seen – the original, Mitchell could talk of 'the relatively few cuts and alterations' in the British version. Not merely the final *dénouement*, but the whole of the

1. Fo in his most celebrated piece: *Mistero buffo*.

2–7: The Fo–Rame partnership in a wide variety of plays:
2. *Settimo: ruba un po' meno (Seventh Commandment: Steal A Bit Less)*, 1964.

3. *La signora è da buttare (The Woman Should Be Kicked Out)*, R.A.I. television, 1977.

4. Rehearsing *Tutta casa, letto e chiesa (Female Parts)* in 1978.

5. *Arlecchino*, 1985.

6. *Clacson, trombette e pernacchi (Trumpets and Raspberries)*, 1981.

7. *Quasi per caso una donna: Elisabetta (Elizabeth, Almost By Accident A Woman)*, 1984.

8. Rame's great breakthrough role: the Mother of Michele Lu
Lanzone in *L'Operaio conosce 300 parole (The Worker Knows
300 Words)*, 1969.

9. Rame in *Una donna sola (A Woman Alone)* from *Female Parts*, 1977.

10. Rame in *Arlecchino*, 1985.

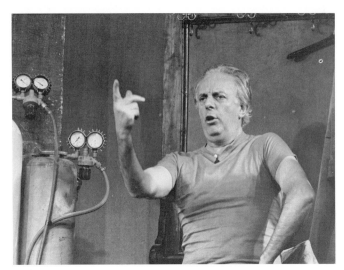

11. Fo as Giovanni in *Non si paga, non si paga! (Can't Pay? Won't Pay!)*. Revival (revised version), 1980.

12. Fo as Arlecchino, 1985.

latter part of the second act, bears no resemblance whatever to the original. It is worth pointing out what Fo wrote.

Giovanni admits his party is wrong in a lengthy confession, the seriousness of which can be judged from his analysis of Moro's famous *compromesso storico* (historic compromise), the idea that Communists and Christian Democrats could work more closely together to achieve their respective aims. Through the mouth of Giovanni Fo pours scorn on this political tactic: 'this flirting with the Christian Democrats in order to get into the government seems to me little more than the tricks of Brighella, who wants a free fuck from a prostitute, only to find he's got free syphilis as well' (*Non si paga*, p. 96). A mordant comment of this nature – characteristically combining Fo's theatrical and political knowledge – is in its trenchant force a world away from anything in the British adaptation.

Giovanni concludes his political *volte-face* by saying, 'Today I really have understood that we have to change the tune. We must be thick-skinned and make sure we reclaim what is ours . . . the only way of making them see reason is to push them down the lavatory and pull the chain' (p. 98). Neither the unrelenting determination nor the style finds any echo in the British version, which can only come up with expressions of solidarity and defiance such as 'get in there, old cock, there's a fight on' and 'we want the bread *and* the biscuits, so shut your cake 'ole'. These phrases belong to the most inept and cheap form of comedy; but we should realise that we are up against something more insidious in the deliberate debasing of Giovanni's language through mixed metaphor and cliché, an effect confirmed by Margherita's incoherent response:

GIOVANNI: Well, we're going to have to pull ourselves
up by the bootstraps, and roll our sleeves up and get
weaving up to our elbows, otherwise someone'll nick
the carpet out from under our feet and we'll be up
the spout without a paddle.

MARGHERITA: I know exactly what I mean.

(*Can't Pay? Won't Pay!* p. 50)

This systematic ridiculing of the worker's intelligence and
will is the exact opposite of Fo's aim and achievement.

All through this final scene there is important offstage
action which is described by the characters on stage. This
gives a wider context and significance to the events taking
place within the domestic situation. The police turn up to
evict all the families who have not paid their rent (they
call on Antonia and Giovanni too) and supervise the
appropriation of their property, which is loaded into large
vans. But the women turn and provoke the police to
gunfire. A boy is shot and carried off. But then the tide
turns and the women start to reclaim their furniture. This
is both an extension of the actions in the supermarket
earlier – again it is the women who take the initiative –
and a reminder of the seriousness of the fight between
workers and the state, the latter represented here by the
police.

Fo gives powerful lyrical expression at the end of the
play to the determination to fight for a better world. There
are echoes here of Bond's technique – in essence a musical
one – which he employs most notably in *Restoration* and
*The Worlds* to give added resonance and depth to working-
class consciousness and will. 'Now we are going to keep
ourselves,' comments Giovanni, 'make our own houses,
invent a new life for ourselves' – and he hymns the vision
of a better world which will be brought about through

solidarity and enlightened socialism. This turns finally into a choric expression of the theme by the whole cast as they advance to the footlights and sing the praises of the worker who will be able to live and die – 'a man who has lived content and free with other men' (*Non si paga*, p. 99). It is a technique Fo borrows from his own drama *L'operaio conosce trecento parole, il padrone mille, per questo lui è il padrone* (*The Worker Knows 300 Words, the Boss 1000; That's Why he's the Boss*), written a few years previously.

British playgoers familiar with the British version of *Can't Pay? Won't Pay!* will recognise none of the above. The Walker adaptation invents instead a series of personal reconciliations between the four principal characters and rewrites the *dénouement* around this sentimental situation. It represents the essence of bourgeois theatre. One begins to see exactly why the play, in this version, has enjoyed such commercial success. That it represents, however, a complete betrayal of Fo – to say nothing of Marx or Gramsci – and has nothing whatever to do with serious political theatre may be judged by measuring its achievement against the 'need to operate collectively' – Fo's approach, as expounded in his introduction to the Italian text:

We have tried to express this in a 'theatre of situation'. That is to say in a technique linked to that of Epic Theatre where the action is not advanced through the characters but through the situation, the plotting. [This implies making] a cultural choice because concerning yourself with a theatre of situation implies presenting a story, not merely acting it. It means not being bothered about the 'drama' that grows out of the individual and his private problems in relation with other people, but,

105

on the contrary, being concerned with the problems of other people within the drama of a group.

(*Non si paga*, p. 5)

# 4
# The Monologues

Io sono convinta che al socialismo noi donne dobbiamo arrivarci tenendo per mano i nostri compagni, o magari portandoceli a calci, ma sempre assieme.

[I'm convinced that when it comes to socialism we women must get there holding our men by the hand, or even kicking them up the arse. But either way, it has to be together.]

(Franca Rame, *Fronte popolare*, 11 Dec 1977)

If Fo's most popular and widely performed plays outside Italy have been the political farces, there remains another area of his work which has developed considerably since the late sixties and which has both furnished him with his own greatest success as an actor and provided an outlet for a much wider appreciation of his work. This is the genre of the dramatic monologue. In 1969 *Mistero buffo* – his own one-man show – burst on the world; in the same year he wrote one of his most politically biting dramas: *L'operaio conosce trecento parole, il padrone mille, per questo lui è il padrone* (*The Worker Knows 300 Words, the Boss 1000: That's Why he's the Boss*), which – in its violent juxtaposition of performance styles – contained the long monologue of the mother of Michele Lu Lanzone: a *tour-de-force* for Franca Rame. This piece also featured in Franca Rame's own show *Parliamo di donne* (*Let's Talk about Women*), which was first produced as a counterpart to *Mistero buffo* when RAI television broadcast several of Fo and Rame's important dramas in 1977. *Parliamo di donne* was soon transformed into *Tutta casa, letto e chiesa* (known in Britain as *Female Parts*), which quickly established itself – as Rame wanted it to – in the repertoire of many actresses. Both *Mistero buffo* and *Female Parts* have opened the way for further explorations of the virtuoso solo piece: in Fo's *La storia della tigre e altre storie* (*The Story of the Tigress and Other Stories*) and *Il fabulazzo osceno* (*Obscene Fables*); and in the monologues about Ulrike Meinhof and Gudrun Ensslin along with the equally intense pieces *Lo stupro* (*The Rape*) and *La madre* (*The Mother*), which have carried Rame's stark revelations of the treatment of women into more powerful and disturbing areas.

Fo and Rame have risen to the challenge of this performance style in markedly different ways. The mixture of savage satire and irreverent comedy which distinguishes *Mistero buffo* gave way to the much more genial humour of *La storia della tigre*. The companion pieces to the latter, which narrate the first miracle of the child Jesus and the stories of Daedalus and Icarus and of Abraham and Isaac with original twists characteristic of the inspired comic genius Fo, are zany narrations which anticipate the scatological excesses of *Fabulazzo osceno*. Rame's development has been in a contrary direction. The humour of *Female Parts*, darkening through each episode and culminating in the rage of Medea in the final monologue, a highly unorthodox handling of the story, has given way to far more dramatic, emotionally intense stories of cruelty and oppression. The lengthy lament of Mary, who curses the Archangel Gabriel for deceiving her when she is faced with Christ's final sacrifice, and the short piece in which she learns (through the conversation of other women and the miraculous imprint on Veronica's handkerchief) that it is her son who has been executed – pieces appended later to *Mistero buffo* – are episodes in a very different key from Fo's own exhuberant narrations. The monologues about the woman who has been raped and physically mutilated (an account based on Rame's own experience) and the mother who learns her son is a terrorist and experiences the pain and humiliation of visiting him in prison take all-too-familiar contemporary realities and force the audience to confront the horror directly.

In fact all of Rame's monologues (with the exception of those in *Mistero buffo*) deal with contemporary issues; Fo's by contrast, are always concerned with the re-creation of events from history, myth or fable. Yet, as we shall see, there is nothing remote about Fo's stories: no hint of historicism. In his retelling of often familiar tales he challenges his audience's views about the past and their own social, political and ethical attitude to their history. His purpose has been very close to that of Mao and Gramsci. As he comments in the introduction to *Mistero buffo*, '[Mao says] that satire is the most efficient weapon the people have in their hands to make them learn (in the context of their own culture) what constitute all the distortions and prevarications imposed on them by their bosses,' (*Le commedie di Dario Fo*, vol. 5, 1977, p. 17). It is the Gramscian approach to history which most particularly distinguishes this work. At the close of the first version of *Mistero buffo* in 1969 Fo quoted these words of Gramsci:

> Knowing yourself means being yourself, means being your own master, knowing who you are, emerging from chaos, being a component of order, but of genuine order and of true discipline to an ideal. And you can't achieve this if you don't know other people as well, their history, the proof of the efforts they have made to be what they are, to create the civilisation they've created and for which we want to substitute our own.   (*Il grido del popolo*, 29 Jan 1916)

By contrast, Rame has tackled contemporary issues head on. There is a directness, a searing force, in her work that we do not find in Fo's, with its propensity to leap from issue to issue, relating them, and forcing us to a fresh evaluation through the power of his wit. Perhaps it is even true to say that, whilst he is essentially a comic actor, unable for long to restrain his exuberant and critical imagination, she is basically a tragic actress, whose burning conviction carries her inexorably from A to Z. Or, rather, it would be truer to say – since neither artist has time for the emotional purgation of tragedy and both have more positive designs on their audience than simply to involve them in a lament for what has been lost – that they are representative of the twin poles of epic theatre. He is the exemplar of Brecht's delight in *Spass* (fun) and *Leichtigkeit* (lightness of touch); she the exponent of his theatre's power to drive straight to the heart of an issue and make the audience through anger will to change what is outmoded and corrupt.

There are few theatrical precedents for these monologues. One may cite the episode of the Jewish Wife in Brecht's *Fear and Misery in the Third Reich*, but it was something quite new for a whole evening to be devoted to such material. Fo's collaboration with Rame – at its most richly expressive and mutually fruitful in this area of their work – and his own pioneer creations are a very far cry from other dramatic monologues one could cite from the modern repertoire. The desperate *cri de coeur* of the woman in Cocteau's *La Voix humaine* and that of the figure in Beckett's *Not I* are expressions of a bourgeois culture at pains to explore the existential *Angst* of the individual. The characters brought to life by Fo and Rame are more than individuals: they are representatives – victims of oppression, exploiters, rulers. They are always seen within a very precisely defined social and political context, so their predicament or situation is related to a much wider set of ethical values. Fo and Rame do not merely live the lives of the characters they are creating: they bring these figures to life with astonishing force and clarity whilst remaining outside their situation – commenting, criticising, demanding something more complex than sympathy: understanding. Yet they demand a full understanding of the circumstances which condition the character's conduct: circumstances, moreover, which can – and must – be changed.

The true precedent for this style of entertainment is to be found in Fo's very first work, *Poer nano* (Poor Kid), a series of monologues performed on Italian radio. This provides the earliest hints of what was to emerge much more fully almost two decades later, as well as harking back to the folk origins of this style of work. In *Poer nano*

Fo was at pains through burlesque to reverse the myths of history and literature purveyed in school. His technique was paradox, presenting the opposite of what was traditional: thus Cain is presented as a victim, not a killer; Othello as an albino who is crazed with anger because Desdemona refuses to flirt with his pal, Iago. Fo learnt these stories, he tells us, from the storytellers (*fabulatori*) of the village on the shore of Lake Maggiore where he was brought up as a child. These fabulous and unorthodox narratives – as well as his own adaptations of them – were, he tells us,

> not merely an end in themselves: they were a sacred refusal to accept the logic of convention; they were a rebellion against the moral assumption that always sees the good on one side and the bad always and only on the other. The enjoyable consolation of upsetting the rules of the game which had been fixed entirely from one point of view – that of the powers that be: Cain is wicked, Abel good; Goliath the tyrant, David the liberator hero, Adam is an idiot, Eve a contriving whore . . . etc., etc. Why? Who told us this? Who established this truth? Where are the witnesses? And what if the opposite were true? Indeed the opposite is undoubtedly the case! Laughter, the liberating force of entertainment, resides precisely in the discovery that the contradictory view stands up far more readily than the commonplace . . . indeed it's truer . . . or at the very least, more believable. But there's also the great pleasure of desecrating, of knocking down the untouchable and sacred monument of hallowed tradition. Everything that revered texts have established, codified, blessed and glorified.   (Introduction to *Poer nano*, p. 5)

Here speaks – quite literally – the iconoclast: the person who is intent on smashing the sacred image. And, if Fo has developed since the early 1950s in replacing what he seeks to destory by a more positive programme of revolutionary change, he is nevertheless a very different artist from, for example, Edward Bond, who, though he seeks to destroy outmoded beliefs, wishes to replace them with a more rational organisation of social and political ethics. Fo, by contrast, has always been something of an anarchist; and this desire to reverse convention is nowhere more comprehensively demonstrated than in the monologues. It is present in the story of Cain and Abel in *Poer nano*, a clear example of the approach and style he was to explore more productively later. In this short story the moral is far from simple. Abel is the sort of boy, handsome, likable, who can turn his hand to anything; Cain, by contrast, can do nothing right. Abel's prayers overheard by the neighbours – 'Oh God who has been so good as to make the sun come up in the morning when it could just as well have risen in the afternoon; who never makes a mistake, cleverly putting the birds who can fly in the air and the fish who can swim in the sea . . . ' – make them comment on his intelligence; but, when Cain prays, all they can do is say how stupid and clumsy he is. When Abel encourages Cain to call up the echo of the well, the noise made by Cain frightens the birds, who had been filled with joy when Abel did the same thing; and, when Cain stoops to stroke the bee who kissed his brother, the same words of endearment cause it to sting him. No wonder, then, that he kills his brother. Fo makes this the credible conclusion of his amusing and touching narrative and in so doing completely reverses tradition.

In this story that is more or less all he is doing; in *Mistero buffo* the challenges to conventional belief –

spiritual, ethical and political – are far more powerful and their effect more subversive of those values Fo considers outmoded and dangerous. In his later work Fo was in fact to approach much closer to the sort of carefully formulated social satire which characterises the English medieval mystery cycles in general and the work of the so-called 'Wakefield Master' in particular. In the Wakefield version of the Cain and Abel story Cain is the critic of the economic system who refuses to pay his tithe and who, in his defiance of the social and political order, is presented as a sympathetic anti-hero. *Mistero buffo* is distinguished by a markedly similar technique of satire.

### 'Mistero buffo'

First performed in 1969, *Mistero buffo* (*Comic Mystery*) is Fo's one-man show based on his own highly original reworking of traditional stories: from the Bible, from ecclesiastical history and from legend. The title is taken from a drama by the Russian playwright Vladimir Mayakovsky, whose life and work were uppermost in Fo's mind in this period (they feature strongly in *L'operaio conosce trecento parole*, written around the same time). Though in dramatic form Fo's *Mistero buffo* is wholly different from Mayakovsky's *Misteriy a-buff*, the Italian dramatist wished to acknowledge the influence of the Soviet artist who had sought to rewrite the sacred issues of history through farce and parody and in so doing represent the proletarian struggle against the forces of repression and tyranny. The title is allusive, and as such no more significant than Fo's own claims for the authenticity of the sources he has adapted in the work. There is no need to be led, as Tony Mitchell is, into a credulous belief that Fo's sources are deeply significant and that he drew heavily on them; or take him to task, as the Italian critic Michele Straniero does in his study *Giullari e Fo*, for playing fast and loose with those sources. The attitude of Chiara Valentini is much more realistic:

> On the origins of the texts for *Mistero buffo* Fo tried serveral times to bluff his audience into believing they were almost exclusively based on authentic material, only slightly reworked. In fact – as he was to admit later – his own contribution was far more significant. In some instances, such as the story of Bonifacio VIII, all he had to go on were a few chronicles of the Veneto which contained brief reference to the Pope's vesting ceremony and to his meeting with Christ, who was so angry he kicked him: mere hints that allowed him to construct his text with virtually complete freedom. He did much the same with the story of the birth of the clown, where, taking his hint from a medieval reference, Fo recounts how the clown was born, employing expressions which appear to be taken straight from the terminology of the country storytellers he knew in his youth. (*La storia di Dario Fo*, 1977, p. 120)

When Fo first began performing these solo pieces – which originally ran for a total of three hours, about a quarter of the running time that would be needed for a performance using all the material he has since created for *Mistero buffo* – he gave them an air of authenticity by lengthy introductions accompanied by slides of medieval paintings and drawings. This procedure, criticised at the time by many of his most ardent admirers, was soon dropped as he discovered a much more original and effective way of presenting the individual monologues.

Now they are framed by *interventi* – discussions of contemporary issues with the audience, satirical vignettes and comic onslaughts on modern monsters, from political leaders to the Pope. These apparent digressions – usually amusingly relevant to the historical issues dramatised in the monologues themselves – have become as entertaining and as significant as the original narratives, and Fo is now able brilliantly to exploit the relationship between the styles and content of the two elements. As the critic Ugo Volli has pointed out in his analysis of *La storia della tigre*, an offshoot of *Mistero buffo*,

> The fact that the explanations are just as entertaining and as warmly applauded as the show-pieces themselves doesn't change the situation. The confrontation of language and dialect [in the *interventi* and the monologues respectively], of direct conversation with the audience in the theatre and the pretence of telling stories to an ideal public, the parody and the use of a variety of vocal effects define perfectly two areas of performance which complement one another, fit together ideally, both provoking laughter and applause simultaneously. (*La repubblica*, 3 Mar 1979)

Fo has learnt how best to present himself and his material through the development of *Mistero buffo* itself and the creation of its two major offshoots in the two decades since its first performance. It seems a matter of small moment to evaluate the relationship between his own invention and his source material. Even the fact that *Moralità del cieco e dello storpio* (*The Morality of the Blind Man and the Cripple*) is based on a story by Andrea della Vigna and *La nascita del villano* (*The Birth of the Villein*) attributed to Matazone de Caligano in no way detracts from Fo's original achievement. He now realises he no longer needs to justify the show by reference to sources and authorities: its performance history has earned it a place in the modern repertoire quite independent of historical and literary precedent. Valentini also points out that Fo was inclined to offer further justification of the worth of the piece by placing it firmly in the tradition of the medieval *giullari* or jesters. This, she argues,

> is one of the typical *a posteriori* justifications Fo tended to employ in one phase of his career: at the beginning of the seventies, when he had the habit of cloaking every single thing he did with a cultural explanation. In fact it was above all Fo's intuitive theatrical knowledge, the enormous experience he had accumulated in twenty years of theatre, moving from the tiny review houses to the big bourgeois theatres and then to the deserted warehouses on the outskirts of Milan, which led him to this solution. Where the Brechtian alienation effect was liberally reinterpreted and soldered to a recouping of popular culture, and where Fo's skill as a narrator of monologues, one he had revealed in *Poer nano* – and one which is part of the tradition of the great variety comedians of Italian review – allies itself to a passionate concern with civil issues and political commitment.   (Valentini, *La storia di Dario Fo*, p. 120)

Despite the truth of Valentini's remarks there is another truth: one revealed in the recent show *Arlecchino* (1985). Fo does feel the need at times to bolster his own skills by reference to his descent from a line of important theatrical pioneers. The brief – and somewhat superficial – introduction to this show, tracing the significance of *commedia dell'arte*, in no way enriched the pieces of

117

clowning which illustrated the tradition. The *lazzi* (set pieces of comic business) and sketches that attempted to re-create *commedia* material were entirely dwarfed by Fo's own stand-up contemporary routines. These parodies and satires of modern Italian life did show the influence of *commedia*, yet by shedding the pseudo-academic trappings employed elsewhere they showed Fo's independence of them and correspondingly gained in seriousness and weight.

It is, in fact, one thing to be aware of your role within a theatrical and historical tradition, but another to parade this too ostentatiously before your audience. In an interview with *Cahiers du cinéma* in 1974 Fo drew attention most pointedly to his relationship with the tradition of *commedia* and the significance of this in the context of his own political aims in creating *Mistero buffo*:

> *Commedia dell'arte* means comedy performed by professionals, those who are recognised as artists. Only artists recognised by the authorities were classed as *commedia* actors. The word *arte* in fact implied the corporation of dramatic arts; it brought together those who were authorised to perform for the counts, dukes, etc . . . Ruzzante, too, at the start was associated with the *commedia*; then he had a crisis at the time of the Anabaptist movement when they tried to liberate the workers – particularly the miners – from being exploited. There was that huge war that Marx and Engels talk about. Ruzzante had a political crisis of conscience and decided to go and perform in public, in the squares. (*Cahiers du cinéma*, no. 250, 1974)

Fo sees himself as a *giullare di piazza* (street entertainer); he wants to reverse the process of history whereby the clown, the *commedia* artist gradually moved away from performing to the people and became a court entertainer, a *buffone di corte*. After the revolutionary movements of the late 1960s he and Franca Rame formed their theatre group Nuova Scena in an effort to place their skills directly at the disposal of the workers' struggle. Fo's creation of *Mistero buffo* was his immediate response to this and most clearly reveals the role he envisaged for his comic skills in the social and political war. His specific aim in *Mistero buffo* is to rewrite history, or, rather, to retell historical events from another point of view: that of the people, so challenging and subverting the official view. As he says in the introduction to the piece about Bonifacio VIII,

> Who organises our culture? Who decides what should be taught? In whose interest is it to keep back certain information? The boss. The bourgeoisie. As long as we go on allowing them to do this, naturally they'll go on doing what they think is right. Just imagine if they took leave of their senses and started telling us how in the fourteenth century in Lombardy and Piedmont there was a real live revolution during which, in Christ's name, they managed to found a community in which everybody was equal, everybody looked after everybody else, there was no exploitation . . . what would happen? Quite probably the kids would go wild and shout, 'Long live Fra Dolcino! Down with the Pope!' You can't allow that, my God, you can't allow that!
>
> (*Le commedie di Dario Fo*, vol. 5, 1977, p. 110)

He goes on to admit that he has seen such revolutionary events mentioned in textbooks – but only as a footnote. It is his aim quite literally to subvert traditional history, to turn it on its head and restore the values of a neglected culture. This Fo undoubtedly achieves in *Mistero buffo*, as Roberto Mutti has most eloquently affirmed:

> The great achievement of Dario Fo has been to rediscover and propose afresh a cultural heritage which has been either forgotten or relegated to the narrow dusty attic of folklore, where the bourgeois bury anything that doesn't fit into their area of control. If it's true, therefore, that 'the dominant culture is the culture of the dominant class' (Marx), it's also true that the oppressed classes have always known how to express though their art a vision of the world with a revolutionary potential. For this reason, *Mistero buffo* is still today – several years after its first performance – a show that has a mass working-class appeal not only with the power to amuse, but also to teach.
>
> (*Fronte populare*, 16 Mar 1975)

In the first version of *Mistero buffo* (reproduced in the Einaudi edition) Fo began with an analysis of a medieval (mid-thirteenth-century) Sicilian poem, 'Rosa fresca aulentissima' ('Sweet-Smelling, Fresh Rose'). His purpose is clear and immediately establishes the aim of the show as a whole. This poem by Cuillo (or Cielo) d'Alcamo is familiar to Italian students as the first flowering of courtly poetry. It is studied in schools and is enshrined as the first poem in Francesco de Sanctis's celebrated two-volume analysis of Italian literature: a critical study published in 1870–1 which, in tracing the origin and development of Italian culture, has been profoundly influential in educational circles. Though de Sanctis states, 'the poem comes out all in one breath, is completely spontaneous, lively, dramatic, light, without a hint of artifice or rhetoric', nevertheless it represents for him the start of a civilised bourgeois culture, being: 'a dialogue between lover and lady [*amante e madonna*], the lover who begs and the lady who keeps denying, and finally gives in'. This is not what Fo believes: he is determined to change the received opinion of this work, to revalue its social and political significance. He argues that it is a much less refined, more bawdy piece, a conversation not between two noble figures but between a tax-collector and a servant girl. The man is trying to pass himself off as a noble and the girl as his mistress. Fo argues that the down-to-earth language undermines the young man's pretence at a lofty style, and that his final argument – that he will if necessary pay her family a *defensa* of 2000 *augustari* – alludes to the custom whereby noblemen paid a fine to the families of girls they had raped in order to escape prosecution. For Fo, this reference clinches the argument that the verses were written by a social critic, a writer wishing to draw attention to political abuses, a man of the people. That his name should be Ciullo (a dialect word for the penis) serves Fo's critical purposes perfectly, as he claims this has been changed in the textbooks to 'Cielo' ('Heaven'). This is what de Sanctis calls him, alluding – significantly enough, in a footnote – to the tendency of modern critics to change his actual name, Ciullo, which is 'of uncertain origin'.

Thus Fo neatly demonstrates precisely how the dominant bourgeois culture has appropriated works in a popular tradition and removed their satiric bite. Much the same thing has happened with English medieval literature and drama. The plays by the Wakefield Master in A. C. Cawley's edition are given little credit as satiric masterpieces clearly directed at the dominant class by a rebel. For instance, Cawley completely misses the biting humour in the *First Shepherd's Play* when the shepherds are obliged to imagine a magnificent feast which is in stark contrast to their own poor provisions. Similarly, he underestimates the satire on the tyrannical powers of contemporary rulers and the significance of the fact that Herod's agents are rewarded, not punished – an ethical point quite at variance with the conventional religious moral of the story. Fo's purpose is to reassess the heritage of popular culture and his task is the more difficult because he is dealing with an essentially oral tradition, one which he is obliged to reconstruct partly from records and texts, but largely through his own imaginative skills as a writer and performer. The popular culture of English medieval drama is there for all to read; Fo had much less to work on in bringing to life the native traditions of his own country, which have been more effectively obscured.

A fine explanation of how he effects this is his own comment on the story of David's drunkenness, an episode, he claims, which was dear to the medieval *giullari*, and notably to one such entertainer, Hans Holden, who was burnt at the stake for defying the Church's prohibitions of his work. This for Fo is the ultimate expression of the repressive power of the state, and at the same time emphasises the equally powerful subversive force of theatre. Fo envisages David – or, rather, the *giullare* taking the role – challenging the *status quo* by claiming that God did not come down to earth to preach fairness and justice: rather he arbitrarily allocated riches and power, telling the people to work for their masters or he would kick them straight to hell. This inversion of Church teaching, with its advocacy of endurance now and promise of compensating rewards in the afterlife, is fully in tune with Fo's Marxist stand. As he has said,

> When I recount how the medieval clown taught people how to interpret the Bible and the gospels, I repeat the

technique of the ancient clown who discovered in certain episodes from the Bible and the gospels the key to his own parables about the external workings of power and of the person who is subject to power . . . I show today's audience what was his method for discovering in the culture of the past – precisely, that is, in the Bible and the gospels – the fate that was in store for him; what was his way of expressing himself through the mouth of the clown; and I invite him to repossess his own culture, to know how to reapproach today that erudite and bookish culture.

(Valentini, *La storia di Dario Fo*, p. 123)

In inverting the morality of traditional biblical stories Fo is combining the secular – and at times the pagan – with the Christian. In his introduction to the story of the wedding-feast at Cana he draws attention to the festivity at Piana dei Greci in Sicily in which Christ is represented as entering Jerusalem along with Bacchus and Dionysus – deities whose cults were subsumed into the Christian faith. In his own version of the turning of the water into wine, Fo opens the story with a confrontation between an angel and a drunkard. The former wishes to give the official version, the latter the popular one. Finally the drunkard upstages the angel and tells – in very down-to-earth terms – how Christ performed the miracle (the wine didn't run out; one of the barrels of wine had turned to vinegar). Christ then climbs on a table – a trifle drunk himself – and instructs the people not to think of the afterlife, but to enjoy themselves whilst they can. He is a reincarnation of Bacchus, the god of wine, and preaches a gospel which is 'exactly the opposite of what we are taught as children when we are told we must endure suffering . . . we're in a vale of tears . . . not everyone can be rich, there are the fortunate and the unfortunate . . . but all will be compensated on the other side' (*Mistero buffo*, p. 55).

Anyone who has visited the Good Friday ceremonies at Trapani, Sicily (they too are termed *misteri*), will recognise this blend of the pagan and the Christian. Twenty huge tableaux of the stations of the cross are carried out of the main church and borne round the city on the shoulders of the hundreds of bearers, who keep this up for twenty-four hours, getting progressively more drunk. The whole city turns out and takes part; each tableau is ornately decorated with flowers and huge candles and accompanied by its own brass band, which intones funeral marches throughout the long night as the passion of Christ is re-enacted and relived by the whole community. Pagan rituals maintain their strongest hold in Sicily and provide a fascinating parallel to Fo's own attempt to re-create native cultural traditions in a genuine and meaningful form.

Fo's piece about Pope Bonifacio VIII is the most celebrated episode in *Mistero buffo* and underlines his, and his public's, relish for demolishing figures of authority. The process begins in the introduction to the piece. Fo describes the lifestyle of Bonifacio, concluding with a reference to a banquet he organised on Good Friday, inviting prostitutes to an orgy which scandalised all the courts of Europe, including the English. This leads him on to a typical comic elaboration which immediately precedes the narration proper:

It's said in fact that in order to entertain his barons at a banquet Henry III [of England] put out a candle with a fart at three yards distance. Someone adds as well – though I don't believe it – that he even managed to do it on the rebound, that is farting towards the wall . . .

124

to one side . . . tac-tac. This is the English sense of humour, and we're not in a position to appreciate all the subtleties, naturally; we have to accept this, it's like cricket. (*Mistero buffo*, p. 111)

Thus the right level has been established for Fo's presentation of the arrogance of the Pope, who tortures his altar-boys (an episode within an episode which yields a brilliantly sustained invention as Bonifacio rehearses the separate voices in the choir) and finally comes face to face with Christ on his way to Calvary. Through the meeting of the two figures Fo effects a confrontation between the arrogance and power of wealth and privilege, on the one hand, and poverty and humility, on the other. His Christ – who does not speak here (or in many of the other stories) – is the revolutionary who comes to bring not peace but a sword. He is the exact opposite of the beautiful loving Christ of a pious tradition, the Christ of Franco Zeffirelli's television film *Jesus of Nazareth*, which profoundly offended Fo. Christ replies to Bonifacio's evasions – his pretence of not having tortured his enemies, of not having nailed to doors the tongues of friars who have spoken against him – by kicking him up the arse. This is Fo's own response to the hypocrisies and tyrannies hallowed by tradition and it is unfailingly the highspot of the show, eagerly awaited and fully appreciated by the audience.

Fo also employs the introductions – more properly the *interventi* or *discorsi*, as they have now become – to place Bonifacio in a more modern context. It was when he narrated the story of the tigress that Fo began most fully to elaborate his highly irreverent portraits of the Pope. At that time (1979) Pope Wojtyła (John Paul II) had just taken up office, and it is fascinating to compare his satire on Wojtyła with that on the two previous popes, Paul VI and John Paul I. The latter was always presented by Fo as an amiable fool, a man prone to making absurd analogies – between the function of petrol in a car and that of the soul in the body, for example – or giving inappropriate homilies such as that on Pinocchio: 'Was Pinocchio a Christian? I've asked a question; I want a reply . . . a Christian made of wood? Wood has a soul? Trees have souls? Has a table a soul? A drawer?' – and so on. This account, punctuated with inane grins and knowing looks as the Pope convinces himself that he has made a really powerful point, is to be contrasted with the story of how the much more serious figure of Paul VI – who never smiled in his life, according to Fo – was given a bicycle by the racing-champion Eddy Merckx. Fo pictures the austere Paul VI creeping out of Castel Gandolfo at dawn to try out the bike without being seen by the Swiss Guards and priests. Unknown to him it has no brakes, and Fo creates a hilarious picture of the Holy Father, his cycle bearing the word 'FIAT' on the front and – in case anybody should think he is sponsored by Agnelli's firm – 'VOLUNTAS TUA' on the back, (the three words mean 'Thy will be done') pedalling down the hill, desperately trying to brake, and ending up a 2000-egg omelette, all white and yellow, the papal colours'.

When Fo turned to satirising Wojtyła his tone was far less genial. There is a much more serious, much darker edge to his caricature, in keeping with Fo's declared dislike of the man. In the *interventi* accompanying the story of the tigress, Fo contents himself with fairly harmless jokes about this Pope's passion for sport, giving a wonderful impression of him skiing, keeping his hands free to bless the public; and of his resemblance to Superman jetting around the world to help the needy. Fo tells how at one point, having arrived in his plane, the

126

Pope disappeared. But, no, he had merely fallen straight down to kiss the earth and leave his print: rather as though he were producing his own version of the Turin shroud. But Fo's satire was hardening even then, as in his version of the Pope's words of advice to the poor of the Third World – 'Stay poor and don't break our balls' – and in the mime of him kissing children as though they were on a production line: this turns into a rugby game with the players dressed as priests and a child serving as the ball, and concludes with the suggestion that the Pope should be called Herod. In recent years – with the revelation of Wojtyła's right-wing political views and his closeness to several Vatican scandals – the attacks have hardened. In a recent performance of *Mistero buffo* Fo compared the temptation of Christ to that of the Pope, concluding that, whereas Christ refused to transport himself from place to place or to reveal any signs of pride, Wojtyła knows better.

This Pope is much closer to Bonifacio than any of the other recent pontiffs, and Fo has not been slow to exploit the cunning parallels he can make between them. All this is done with a disarming manner, his satire prefaced by the disclaimer 'Of course our present Pope is nothing like Bonifacio', but his *coup de théâtre* is to confuse their names at one point in such a way that it appears a complete slip of the tongue, an appalling irreligious gaffe. Fo can still shock through these digressions which are in fact to the point. When asked by a reviewer why he took delight in mocking the Church, his answer was clear:

The sacred is one of the great inventions of the world's hypocrisy to prevent the humble from retaining any dignity. The 'sacred' is a limit, a closed door, a taboo to exclude the rest. So then desecration means rooting out this hypocrisy to allow others, more humble, to get closer. I desecrate the figure of the Pope on the basis of what I've read and observed and I depict his arrogance and aggression.

I recount – laying it on with a trowel – the infamy of the killer who attempted to destroy that magical image of his almost baroque identity.   (*Moda*, 2 Nov 1985)

The description of the televised meeting of the Pope and his would-be assassin is indeed a triumph of sustained irony, sealed by Fo's assertion that the tasteful simplicity of the decor was obviously the work of Zeffirelli.

The method of presenting Bonifacio is in some crucial respects different from the narrative technique of the other pieces in *Mistero buffo*. Fo plays the part of Bonifacio, albeit making it clear through his own brand of epic acting that he is presenting the figure for critical analysis. In one sense, therefore, the virtuoso element that distinguishes Fo's acting is less pronounced in this monologue. He is not telling a story in the third person, though the acting style is fully in accord with Brecht's concept of acting in the third person – of presenting objectively rather than identifying subjectively. When talking about the narrative of the wedding-feast at Cana, Fo drew attention to the baisc feature of his narrative style in making it clear that, though the piece opens with a conversation between two figures – the angel and the drunkard – this is more effectively presented, paradoxically, through the monologue than through the dialogue form. He explains,

I perform this piece alone, though not through an excess of exhibitionism. We tried to do it with two actors, but we discovered it didn't work. Because just about all these texts were written to be performed by a solo actor.

The *giullari* worked almost exclusively on their own: we notice this when we observe that in the text everything is achieved by allusion, through doubling up and through hints. So that as a result of the play of imagination the poetic force and the comic strength of the work are doubled. (*Mistero buffo*, p. 55)

Fo adds, meaningfully, that the technique is the exact opposite of the naturalism of the television medium, where the viewer is provided with all the details and can watch, half asleep, without becoming imaginatively involved as a participator – 'so that the day after you're ready to go to work, with nothing in your head, ready to be exploited all over again'. Fo's style in *Mistero buffo* is non-naturalistic; it requires active participation by the audience, who are required to respond to the performer's versatility and the speed with which he can manipulate their responses in making swift changes of perspective.

This is nowhere more exhilaratingly achieved than in the narrative of the raising of Lazarus, where Fo takes on the roles of a whole gallery of figures, switching from a mercenary gatekeeper to a man renting chairs, a sardine-seller, different members of the public jostling and arguing among themselves, and ending with the cries of someone was has been robbed whilst his attention was on the miracle. This is a deeply secular piece, its focus of attention not the miracle itself but the crowd observing it. When Christ arrives with the disciples, one of the crowd waves to Mark as an old friend; when Lazarus rises from the dead (thus confounding the punters who have laid bets against it) one of the observers notices only the rotting condition of the body and the offensive smell.

In Fo's version of the Massacre of the Innocents the women are presented initially as tough mothers, fighting for the lives of their children and abusing the soldiers violently. The killers in their turn are presented as men who argue about the morality of what they are doing, the most cynical pointing out that they pillage and rape in war; this massacre is a no less politically motivated affair. The viewpoint here – both that of the women and that of the men who abuse them – has much in common with the presentation of this story in the Wakefield cycle. Again, no stress is placed on the idea of sacrifice, no time is wasted on pity; the social and political realities are insisted on instead.

When we turn to Fo's account of the madman at the foot of the Cross, a narrative added in later versions of *Mistero buffo*, we can observe further links between Fo's dramatic skill and the technique of artists – both visual and theatrical – during the Middle Ages. The piece is deeply pagan, blasphemous in tone: the Fool – a figure closely resembling the savage clowns created by the Wakefield Master: Mak the sheep-stealer, and Pikeharness in the *Buffeting* play – has bought the body of Christ from the soldier for the thirty pieces of silver he found near the tree on which Judas hanged himself. Subsequently, however, he rejects Christ when he says he wishes to die to redeem the world, adding that the only time he really admired Jesus was when he drove the traders from the temple. Fo's 'o'er-licensed fools' take up precisely the attitude of those figures in the miracle-play tradition who – in their mingling of pagan and Christian values – were so strongly to influence Shakespeare and other dramatists of the Elizabethan period. The opening of this particular narrative has further parallels with the popular art of the medieval period in that we see the men erecting the Cross going about their work and making bets as to how many hammer blows will be necessary to sink the nails. This has some of the sadistic savagery of the Wakesfield Master's account of the Crucifixion, where the workmen are actually called 'torturers' and delight – as do Fo's figures – in tormenting their victim; but Fo is closer to the York version (on which the Wakefield account is based), where the traditional focus on Christ's sacrifice has shifted to a presentation of crucifixion as a job of work – a change of perspective that has all the power of Brecht's *Verfremdungseffekt*, and indeed functions in Fo's drama with the same force.

It is also a technique employed by the Pollaiuolo brothers in their painting *The Martyrdom of St Sebastian* (National Gallery, London), where the picture is dominated by the archers in the foreground, and the background presents a very precisely detailed contemporary landscape. The emphasis is therefore entirely on the social: the figure of the martyr virtually disappears out of the top of the frame. There are other telling parallels with Fo's art. The simplicity of Giotto: notably in the expressive force of the angels bewailing the death of Christ in the *Deposition* in the Scrovegni Chapel, one of them drawing our attention by his upraised clenched fists; or the moving sense of social conditions in Masaccio's religious frescoes: notably the animalistic features of the beggar and the coarse bare bottom of the child resting on its mother's arm in *The Distribution of the Tribute Money* in the Brancacci Chapel. It could be argued that the style of the Chester cycle in its effective simplicity with its striking human touches (as in the celebrated *Noah* play) is very close to that of Giotto, an exact contemporary; and that the technique of the Wakefield Master – in its telling emphasis on suffering figures caught in a precisely defined social situation – employs effects which have much in common with the style of Masaccio. Fo, in recognising the skill of both these artists, enables us to evaluate his own work in a wider cultural perspective.

It was during his protracted argument with Zeffirelli over the merits of *Mistero buffo* as against *Jesus of Nazareth* – a debate which was given maximum press coverage in Italy in 1977, when the two works were televised in close proximity – that Fo drew attention to the significance of these two painters. In defending his version of the story of the raising of Lazarus he pointed out that down-to-earth details of his portrayal were in the same tradition: 'You see it in the paintings of the great popular artists: Giotto, Masaccio, the Lorenzetti brothers: people block their noses; women vomit. Zeffirelli never considers this for a moment. There's neither stench nor people; just a pretty picture.' And he added, citing Pasolini as another artist who (in *The Gospel according to Matthew*) had created a Christ with whom he could sympathise, 'The howling, the cursing in Masaccio is never the subject of Zeffirelli's version, whilst Pasolini didn't take Masaccio as his mentor by accident. He makes him cry, he makes him howl: his is a Christ who goes about blaspheming, who insults people' (*Corriere della sera*, 22 Apr 1977).

'My Christ has more imagination' was the headline that announced Fo's initial attack on Zeffirelli's work. In *Mistero Buffo*, he stressed,

> viewers will find themselves in front of a Christ very much outside the conventional tradition: a Christ who laughs, has a ball, sings, even dances. An exuberant character who slaps his friends on the back so soundly he nearly brings on heart attacks. A Christ who invites the wedding-guests at Cana to drink his wine, to be happy, to let themselves go, have fun . . . but *now* . . . not to wait until after death in the other world to enjoy

paradise . . . You will have noticed that Zeffirelli in his Christ spectacular has entirely censored the scene of the marriage feast . . . How could he tell the story of a Christ who rolls up his sleeves and produces wine for everyone? His Christ (the creation of someone teaching the catechism) is a huge, saintly Indian-style Christ whose fingers vibrate like those of a guru seized by cathartic trembling every time he's about to perform a miracle.   (*La repubblica*, 22 Apr 1977)

There is more to Fo's attack than personal abuse: Zeffirelli's Christ – in a version of the gospels which was transmitted to a vast audience – was, in Fo's opinion, only serving to bolster the power of Church and state, and represented as much a political gesture as Fo's in creating *Mistero buffo*. In his view, *Jesus of Nazareth* was the expression of a reactionary ethic.

It was precisely on this issue that Zeffirelli most strongly took him to task, arguing that it was all very well for Fo – 'an old man dressed in jeans' – to 'run after the latest intellectual trend for fear of missing the last train of the *contestazione* [see Chapter 5]': he could preach as he liked to his minority audience, but it was another thing to do it on television. 'I insist on saying', argued Zeffirelli, 'that Fo's theatre needs a certain amount of cultural preparation, which it is absurd to expect of the viewing public. So the broadcast ought to have been better prepared and thought out more carefully'. (*La repubblica*, 24 Apr 1977). His argument is an essentially elitist one, precisely propounding that view of culture which Fo is at pains to subvert. Zeffirelli's argument is very like that of Pamela Hansford Johnson in her attack on Bond's *Saved* as pornographic: she argued that it should be banned not to all but to those whose defective education might render them susceptible to its message. Both arguments cloak a more reactionary stand: a determination to protect outmoded and privileged positions. Fo was quick to see the flaw in Zeffirelli's argument, pointing out not only that *Mistero buffo* had played to over a million and a half people, many of them workers, but adding,

> This hypocrisy is absurd. We've come to the point where it is right to give freedom not to everyone but only to those who are worthy of it and prepared. It's the attitude of a coloniser: i.e. the people are like oxen and we should feed them only on grass.
>
> *(Il messaggero, 24 July 1977)*

Zeffirelli's attack on Fo's work succeeded only in drawing attention to its dangerously provocative nature and to the establishment's anxiety about its influence on popular opinion and on attitudes to power and privilege. Zeffirelli lined himself up with the diehards of the Christian Democrat Party and the Vatican, whose newspaper *L'osservatore romano* stigmatised *Mistero buffo* as 'in the last analysis returning to that strategy of ideological violence which has as its first target the religious values of the Italian people but is really aiming at producing the disintegration of the entire Italian state' (quoted in *Avvenire*, 24 Apr 1977). In one respect the newspaper was right: Fo would have rejoiced had he been able, in a single television transmission, to effect such a change in the Italian people. Replying to the accusation that his own narratives brought to mind the Nazis burning books and the Fascists attacking *L'osservatore romano*, he pointed out,

> if I were them, I'd be more wary about evoking violence, burning, the stake and such things. It's they who have

134

always been the first to want to burn, to block, to destroy. Shutting the mouths, indeed pulling out the tongues of all those who try to have a critical debate about power and the arbitrary exercise of power is one of their favourite tricks, a characteristic borne out by history.  (*Il messaggero*, 24 July 1977)

Once again he found himself the butt of savage attacks from outraged individuals who wished to censor or silence him. It had the uncomfortable and yet reassuring ring of history repeating itself. It recalled the events of a decade before which had provoked him and Franca Rame to stop acting as 'jesters to the bourgeoisie' and attempt – with all the protest they inevitably stirred up – to address themselves to a wider audience. As Fo pointedly concluded in his debate with Zeffirelli,

I end reminding Zeffirelli, but not just him, of a phrase from the screenplay of Dreyer's *Jesus*. The film was never made, as we know. One of Jesus's disciples says, 'So long as Jesus attacked the sages and the learned men inside the synagogues, nobody ever bothered him, but, when he went on top of the mountain in order to make his voice carry as far as possible and so that the millions finally (and I stress: finally) could hear him, the powers-that-be began to realise that there was a man to get rid of as quickly as possible.  (*Ibid.*)

### 'The Story of the Tigress'

Fo followed *Mistero buffo* with another evening of monologues when he produced *The Story of the Tigress and Other Stories* (*La storia della tigre e altre storie*), an

135

entertainment which reached its definitive form in 1980. Four years previously Fo had visited China, and there he had been impressed by a peasant *fabulatore* who told a story, in dialect, the gist of which he could understand. He adapted this tale, expanding it from its original fifteen minutes to three times that length, thus producing his longest single monologue. In a programme which included an account of the first miracle of the infant Jesus (taken from the apocryphal gospels of the second and third century) as well as highly unconventional versions of the stories of Daedalus and Icarus and of Abraham and Isaac – the whole linked with irreverent *interventi* about the Papacy – he succeeding in moulding a true sequel to *Mistero buffo*.

This was the first programme I saw Fo perform and the impression it made was a powerful one. Like *Mistero buffo* this has been recorded, but unlike *Mistero buffo* it has been published in an edition which contains lengthy stage directions and attempts to give some impression on the printed page of the vast range of sounds and movements employed by Fo in the performance. Accordingly, a brief account of this work in some detail will serve to give an idea of the artistry and versatility of Fo, unmatched in performances of his monologues by other performers.

Fo begins with an outline of the earlier part of the story, which enables the audience afterwards to enter into the narrative more easily. It is performed in Fo's familiar invented dialect, though Fo, after telling the audience how comprehensible the original Chinese narrator he witnessed was, and what similarities there appeared to be between his dialect and Fo's, announces that he is going to perform in Chinese. Nothing would suprise Fo's audiences, but this is a typical trick to test their response and to win them over with an initial practical joke. Before beginning the narrative proper, Fo explains the message of the story. There is no attempt to mystify the audience: as with the parable which closes *Abbiamo tutte la stessa storia* (*The Same Old Story*), it is important that the audience do not waste time puzzling out the meaning, but spend all their energies concentrating on the way the story is told. The moral of the story, we are informed, is contained in the significance of the tiger in Chinese culture. To possess a tiger implies to go on struggling, not to give in, despair or abandon the fight. It also implies not delegating, but always accepting responsibility. 'Possessing the tiger', says Fo, 'means making sure you are right inside any situation, participating, checking what is going on, verifying things, being present and responsible right down to the last detail' (*La storia della tigre*, 1980, pp. 8–9). This group of narratives in general – and the story of the tigress in particular – is concerned to counter the escapism which Fo observed in society: from the recourse to endless foreign travel to the belief in UFOs. The story, though one of the most entertaining pieces in his repertoire, has a relevance which is not confined to China.

The story is told by a soldier fighting in China against the forces of Chiang Kai-shek who, after a long and intense march, is wounded. When gangrene sets in, his comrades abandon him, though one of them, Fo ironically remarks, offers to shoot him as his suffering is causing them all great pain. A heavy rainstorm makes him take shelter in a cave and it is there that he encounters the tigress and her cub. Fo mimes the soldier's initial terror, which gives way to fascination as the tigress forces him to drink her milk: only one of her cubs has survived, so she must find another creature to suckle. This gives Fo the opportunity for a plethora of sound-effects: the roar of the tigress, the howls of the cub, and the sounds of suckling as the soldier becomes drunk with the milk he is forced to suck from one teat after another. In return the tiger sucks his wound and cures it, but the soldier has problems when the cub – a character rapidly taking on a leading role in the drama – copies his mother but is less careful with his teeth. This obliges the soldier to hit out at the young cub's testicles to keep him in place, and in a hilarious section Fo, arms and legs rigid, walks on all fours in imitation of the cub with his legs crossed, seeking to avoid any further blows.

The tigress goes out and returns later with her spoils: various large animals which are torn apart and devoured to suitable sounds of rending flesh accompanied by grunts and howls of approval. Fo goes on to mime the soldier's own disgust at this devouring of raw meat and explains how he made a fire, collected wild herbs and cooked the food for himself. The cub is naturally the first to try out the new fare, followed shortly by his mother. This sets a new fashion and the soldier is obliged to bully the cub into collecting the fuel and herbs. He soon tires of playing the cook and housewife and, during another deluge, creeps away. There are two very funny moments: the sneaking delight of the young cub, who tells his mother the soldier is making his escape, and the conversion of his mime of swimming away into the insulting Italian gesture expressive of 'Up yours!' He escapes to a village – at first terrorising the natives, who think, because of his appearance (red from the fire and black from the smoke of the cooking), that he is the figure of death. He quickly washes and puts them right, explaining what has happened to him. This is the cue for one of Fo's most bravura exercises: a rapid recapitulation of the whole story, complete with sound-effects (gun-shots, animal noises, and so on). This is rattled off in what Fo terms 'semi-gramelot': a cross between speech and onomatopoeic sounds. Fo employs 'gramelot' in several other narratives and has, indeed, perfected several short pieces entirely in this nonsense language. He explains it as a cunning device invented by comedians in the Middle Ages to avoid censorship. Whilst it is perfectly clear what is being represented, there are no words which can be clearly identified. The power of this technique is seen in Fo's impersonation of an English lawyer successfully defending a nobleman who has committed rape, as well as in his gramelot of the American technocrat. In neither of these pieces does Fo employ recognisable words, but every nuance of the conversation is meaningful. His parody of American speech has been known to cause great offence to dignitaries who felt they were being satirised but were unable to say precisely how.

The soldier stays with the villagers and the tigers find him there. There is a touching scene of reconciliation, and then the tigress and cub, taking care to keep their claws well retracted (Fo mimes all this with relish) are accepted by the village as the children climb onto their backs and are taken for rides. Soon a messenger comes with news of the approach of Chiang Kai-shek's soldiers, but with the help of the tigers, who mount the hill and issue loud roars, the enemy is frightened away. The news travels fast and the village finds itself under pressure to hire out the tigers to their neighbours. Accordingly, they begin a training-programme in which people are taught to put on masks and imitate the tigers. This gives rise to a whole section in which Fo runs through a vast range of howls and roars, organising the whole affair like an orchestral conductor.

Soon the enemy soldiers are a thing of the past and a party representative comes to congratulate the people on their initiative, adding, however, that, since the tigers are no longer needed, and because they lack any sense of dialectical argument, they are no use to the party and must be sent away. The people promise to do this, but install them instead inside chicken coops. This gives Fo the opportunity to extend his zany humour – the epithet takes on added significance when we realise its origins in the comedy of the fool Zanni – by miming the tigers holding one leg up like a hen, emitting sounds which are their impression of a cockerel, and capping this with the idiotic response of the official who thinks he is hearing a 'gallo tigrato' (tiger-cock). The village is threatened by more attacks and the party realises it has disobeyed. The climax – and the crunch – of the story comes when a whole delegation visits the village to repeat the message of congratulation and state that the tigers must be placed in a zoo. As a leading bureaucrat spouts a stream of familiar party gobbledegook, the tigers on cue put an end to this threat by one final and gigantic roar.

### 'Female Parts'

The English title of the monologues written for Franca Rame by Dario Fo immediately alerts us to a rather crucial shift of emphasis in the translation of the work from Italy to Britain. The original title is *Tutta casa, letto e chiesa*, literally *She's All Home, Bed and Church*, and plays on the colloquial Italian phrase *tutto casa, lavoro e chiesa* ('all home, work and church') used to describe the conventional petit-bourgeois Italian. The English title is a trifle unfortunate with its echoes of both feminist and sexist cliché and was quickly modified by the National Theatre with the addition of the mollifying sub-title *One-Woman Plays*. These pieces are far and away the best-known work of Fo and Rame in Britain as they have been performed (and often adapted) by a wide variety of actresses since they were premiered by Yvonne Bryceland at the National Theatre on 26 June 1981. When Franca Rame herself performed the work in London (at the Riverside Studios) the following year, she was the first of the team to appear in Britain, followed shortly by Fo in his version of *Mistero buffo*.

The genesis of these pieces can be traced back to 1977 and to the retrospective of Fo's work assembled by RAI television. In recognition of the significance of Rame's role in the partnership, two of the programmes focused on her work, in a medley of pieces, old and new, collected under the title *Parliamo di donne* (*Let's Talk about Women*). These pieces ranged from variety sketches (including the one in which Fo as a ferocious anti-abortionist finds himself pregnant) to epic monologues (most notably that of the mother of Michele Lu Lanzone, taken from the earlier drama *L'operaio conosce trecento parole*). The programmes hinted at Rame's emergent political militancy and provided the jumping-off point for what was to become her challenge to *Mistero buffo*. At the same time, however, this was an initial, somewhat tentative, exercise, limited both by its character as a compilation of Rame's work over a lengthy period and by the medium for which it was conceived – as Valentini observes:

Let us turn to the second type of dependence on the medium of television the show inevitably encountered: the attempt – of necessity limited and partial – to stitch together a number of female roles was brought about at the price of a certain over-formal schematisation, almost – it seemed – out of a fear that more in-depth analyses might have upset the indifferent television public. Several commentators – and in particular the feminist collectives – weren't slow to criticise the authors for the unusual caution of the text, whilst there were murmurs of disapproval from admirers who felt that *Parliamo di donne* consisted essentially of putting on the stage female characters without, however, confronting the specific issues affecting the problems of women. (Valentini, *La storia di Dario Fo*, 1977, p. 174)

Accordingly, later that year, on 6 December, Rame opened in *Tutta casa, letto e chiesa* at the Palazzina Liberty. This new show contained one piece from *Parliamo di donne*, *Il risveglio* (*Waking Up*); the three other pieces which go to make up the British version of *Female Parts*; and *La mamma frichettona* (*The Freaky Mother*), a mother's confession (on the run from the police) to a less than fully attentive priest of how she has become involved in the punk movement through trying to help her son. This piece soon dated (like the movement itself) and was dropped. Several other, more disturbingly violent, political pieces, such as the monologue of Ulrike Meinhof or that of the prostitute in prison, included in an appendix to the published text and performed in earlier versions of the show, paved the way for the two monologues which form the second part of *Coppia aperta* (*The Open Couple*), but were not for long included in *Tutta casa*. Neither was *Contrasto ad una voce sola* (*Duet for One Voice*), tried out in a new version of the show in 1981. It involved the (silent) participation of an actor as the lover who has been brought back secretly to his woman's home, but it lacked the force and relevance of the other monologues.

More significantly, this 1981 version of the show began with an introduction which Rame has retained and developed. This is very much the equivalent of Fo's

142

*discorsi* in *Mistero buffo*: it sets the tone and themes of the show very clearly, wittingly raising a number of crucial issues in relation to the feminist viewpoint on sex and gender, as well as disarming potential misinterpretation of the succeeding pieces from the start. Since this introduction has – most regrettably – been omitted from the British version, it is worth emphasising its function and significance before examining the individual monologues in more detail.

Rame begins by announcing, with suitable ironic force, that 'the sole protagonist of this show about women is the man'. She goes on to talk about the taboos, verbal and social, which constrict women, and goes straight to the heart of the matter by discussing the way in which language inevitably consolidates – and creates – sexist attitudes. She expresses annoyance at her difficulty in bringing herself to use the word *cazzo* ('prick') and bemoans the fact that men have replaced God with their private organ in substituting the expression 'Oh! cazzo!' for the once equally commonplace 'Oh! mio dio!' This is light-hearted, but there are serious political implications in the fact that, conversely, 'if our sex has to be named – in rape cases, for instance – Latin is used: a dead language – *Cunno, cunna, cunnis*, third declension and irregular'. Relishing the gap between sex and gender (which is non-existent in English), Rame goes on to bemoan the situation of the 'female eunuch': the lack of a tail (ironically '*la* coda' in Italian), the specific attribute of the male tiger (again, '*la* tigre' in Italian). Her wordplay here brings to mind the amusing change in gender which the word *tigre* underwent in Italy when the celebrated advertisement for petrol instructed the car-owning public, 'Put a tiger in your tank.' Overnight the force of the publicity campaign – and more significantly, the macho implications of the

Dario Fo and Franca Rame

slogan – changed the gender of the animal: it became '*il* tigre'.

Rame has a great deal of fun with language in her introduction when she moves on to illustrate the power of masculine sexual language against its feminine equivalent. The historical tradition of macho arrogance is mocked while at the same time its implications are implicitly accepted. Ignorant travesties of language do nothing to fight the battle against misguided and outmoded sexist attitudes; these are best fought by exposing them directly for what they are. This Rame achieves brilliantly in her parody of two styles of heroic writing, the one Homeric and militaristic, exploiting the full power of the masculine attributes; the other Danteesque, revealing the inadequacy of the vocabulary relating to female sexuality. She contrasts

> Came the most high Hermes,
> Before him, armed,
> His helmet raised in front,
> The undefeated PREPUCE
> Next to his brother GLANS,
> Magnificent, surmounting the pounding SCROTUM
> Erecting amidst the standards of war his PENIS
> For the thrusting hero

with the 'horrible, disgusting' terms associated with women:

> The bats were flying at twilight,
> The VAGINAS were croaking in the swamp.
> It was the hour of the depositing of the OVARIES.
> A UTERUS – enormous – rose up in the night:

The SPERMATOZOA all died of terror.
(*Tutta casa, letto e chiesa*, 1981, pp. 5–9)

Rame's introduction is deliberately shocking, provocative; women are not supposed to employ such language, let alone make fun of it. She and Fo, however, are in the tradition of entertainers such as Lenny Bruce, who, by deliberately addressing members of his audience as 'spicks', 'grease-balls' and 'kykes', underlined the added force given to language when it is repressed.

Confronting, not avoiding, the issues has been the technique of Fo and Rame throughout their career in the theatre. In the later London performances of *Tutta casa*, Rame took it upon herself to harangue those feminist critics in Britain who had objected on principle to her appearance in a see-through negligée in *Una donna sola* (*A Woman Alone*). This is a precisely parallel issue to the one concerning language. The situation of the petit-bourgeois woman indoctrinated by the mass media and reduced to a sex object by all the men around her is one of which Rame, as a celebrated and glamorous actress (notably in her career in revue and television in the late fifties and early sixties), is well aware. She exploits her own sexuality on stage in the battle against sexism. As the critic representing *Il manifesto* (Italy's most sophisticated and outspoken Marxist newspaper) aptly commented in reviewing *Tutta casa*,

> To bring this off, Franca Rame has made a very deliberate choice, and is to be congratulated on her success. She has gone back and made use of her past career as a great comic actress – her ingenuous cunning and her charms as a soubrette – with all the discernment of her present militant position. She has brought to

145

fruition the experience and the techniques of Dario Fo, including the work on television last year. The result is the undeniable entertainment value which at the beginning of the show in particular is in full evidence. (*Il manifesto*, 28 Nov 1978)

Rame's own attitude to feminist politics is significant. It is well summed up in the interview she granted *Il manifesto* just before *Tutta casa* opened:

One must take one's hat off to what the feminist movement has achieved. Feminists have made so many people understand so many things, and, thanks to their efforts, I too have a different relationship with my family. I, however, believe that the new condition of women depends on the transformation of society. First we have to change class relationships: I believe women's liberation is tied to the class struggle. And, as well, we need to change men, make them learn to discover and respect our dignity. Then finally women will be really free. (*Il manifesto*, 25 Nov 1977)

The sophistication of Rame's approach – which unites a deeply political motivation with an awareness of her own sexual attractiveness and her love for men – is not always present in the more puritanical atmosphere of feminist and left-wing politics in Britain.

The other feature of Rame's introduction which links it to Fo's technique in *Mistero buffo* is the clear-cut synopsis of the stories before they are performed, with explicit explanation of their significance. This is particularly revealing in the case of *Abbiamo tutte la stessa storia* (*The Same Old Story*), where the scabrous fairy tale at the end is explained so that there can be no misunderstanding of its meaning. This removes from the audience the need to agonise about the interpretation: they can concentrate instead on the skills of the narrative technique. Rame states,

> We have a splendid little girl, beautiful, blonde, blue-eyed, and a rag-doll who talks dirty. These two figures are we women ourselves. The sweet little girl is that part of us which is docile, which gives in, which accepts; the doll, by contrast, represents our rebellion. The 'red cat' is our companion. The 'wolf' represents all those male figures who oppress us right from infancy: father, brother, head of the office, etc. Then we grow up, the two parts intermingle, we become a single entity, there follows maturity and the taking of a moral stand.
>
> (*Tutta casa*, p. 12)

It is a pity that this is missing from the British version; it would have prevented a good deal of misinterpretation. On the subject of the reception of the narrative and the way women – as against men – immediately glimpse its significance, Rame relates how when the piece was first performed only the women laughed, and delighted shouts of 'I recognise you, you idiot!' (addressed to boyfriends, fiancés and husbands) resounded through the theatre. Real arguments broke out, and subsequently it was observable that men were laughing too. Rame's comment on the significance of this is salutary:

> But take note, you women here in the theatre, the male's laugh has nothing human about it! They laugh out of time, they laugh without reason. And then they come out with a really fantastic remark: 'I'm laughing because I'm not one of them over there. I'm a feminist

too!' As far as I'm concerned the feminist male ought
to be strangled at birth.   (Ibid, p. 11)

Despite these similarities of technique to *Mistero buffo* –
chiefly evident in the introduction – *Female Parts* employs
narrative devices which are very different from those used
by Fo in his celebrated monologues. In all four of the
pieces which make up the British edition, the actress is
asked to assume a character: the woman desperately
preparing to go to work, the housewife threatened by a
variety of male oppressors, the woman who bears an
illegitimate child, and Medea. In the various Italian
versions Rame has added to this repertoire at times the
punk mother, the woman who has secretly smuggled her
lover into the house, Ulrike Meinhof and the imprisoned
prostitute, plus the mother who visits her terrorist son in
prison and the woman who has been raped: the subjects
of the second part of *Coppia aperta*. The rape victim
presents a particularly extreme example of role creation:
the actress had herself suffered the experience that she
here turns into a theatrical piece. The difference between
the monologues performed by Fo and those enacted by
Rame is in the nature of the epic theatrical techniques
employed. Only in the case of Bonifacio VIII does Fo
impersonate a single character, and Bonifacio is presented
with an intense degree of critical objectivity. By contrast
Rame plays the individuals central to her stories and in
so doing demands a much greater level of sympathy for
them. Fo prefers to portray a galaxy of figures – in
*Resurrezione di Lazzaro* (*The Raising of Lazarus*) and
*Strage degli innocenti* (*The Massacre of the Innocents*), for
example – or to present a dialogue, as in *Le nozze di Cana*
(*The Marriage at Cana*) and *Moralità del cieco e dello
storpio* (*The Morality of the Blind Man and the Cripple*).

Rame's different technique is evident in *Passione. Maria alla croce* (*The Complaint of Mary beneath the Cross*) in *Mistero buffo* and can be traced back to the impassioned outburst of the mother of Michele Lu Lanzone.

This is not to imply, however, that Rame's monologues are naturalistic. She presents the individuals; she does not immerse herself in them; there is nothing of what the Italians term *immedesimazione*: total identification with the role in the manner of Stanislavsky or the Method school. There is a fundamentally different theatrical process at work in Rame's performances, which is intimately bound up with the fact that she is demanding a more intense emotional response from her audience, requiring them to enter more completely into the situation so that they may be the more disturbed, the more inclined to respond and change matters. Fo exhibits a stunning versatility in shifting from role to role, a seemingly endless imaginative response to the rapidly changing situations he is presenting; Rame, by contrast, requires a more difficult reaction which involves both sympathy and judgement. Both actors are employing devices characteristic of Brecht's epic theatre, but, whereas Fo is the born comic, Rame is closer to the Brecht who said, expressing the limitations of naturalistic theatre,

> Probably you'll have repeatedly to get inside the person you are representing, his situation, his physical characteristics, his modes of thought. It's one of the operations involved in building the character up. It's entirely consistent with our purposes, so long as you know how to get out of him again. (Bertolt Brecht, (*The Messingkauf Dialogues*, 1965, p. 55)

This Rame succeeds in doing with remarkable skill.

149

Whether presenting the trials of a working woman, the dilemma of a middle-class victim of a male-dominated society, the problems of a more articulate woman, or the reactions of the regal Medea, she shifts her point of focus constantly, thus alternately drawing us into the situation and forcing us to take stock of it. Ugo Volli has succinctly summed up the differences between her style and Fo's:

> Franca Rame performs alone on stage for two hours twenty minutes, and the obvious parallel seems to be with *Mistero buffo*; but there isn't any real resemblance. Not so much on account of the presence of stage furniture, or the see-through nightie or the gipsy costume Rame is dressed in, but on account of the basic dramatic structure of the pieces. Pretending all the time to be talking to someone who can't be seen (the child, a more-or-less indifferent neighbour, a priest who's half asleep) what Rame's women produce is a stream of consciousness, an internal monologue, a chatty confession, full of new twists and turns, unable to be pinned down, sweeping you away with it. Mingling actual events and psychological insights, it alternates between descriptions of what's happening on stage, and comments, explanations, political analyses, memories relived with the same immediacy as present events, and associations of ideas.   (*La repubblica*, 6 Dec 1977)

The ordering of the pieces in the British version (coupled with the omission of those monologues which Rame had tried out and dropped from the show) can give the impression that there is a deliberate development from an inarticulate worker through to a highly politicised ruler as we move from the woman of *Waking Up* through to Medea. Furthermore, the emphasis of two of the pieces,

*The Same Old Story* and *Medea*, is changed in the translation. For *Medea* Rame adopted an accent of central Italy, the regions of Umbria and Tuscany, so as to produce a more down-to-earth figure of popular tradition whose motives are very different from those of the protagonist of Euripides' tragedy. Again, a lengthy introduction to the piece (cut in the British version) makes it clear that the point of the story is 'not jealousy or rage but a new awareness, the taking of a moral stand'. This morality – shocking in the event – deliberately follows the stand taken by the woman in *The Same Old Story*, who, rejecting abortion because of the expense, raises her child (a girl) on a story of female vengeance following a growing awareness of her situation. Medea's decision to kill her children thus becomes the ultimate feminist blow: the refusal to accept the yoke which a male-dominated society has forced her to wear.

Another aspect of translation affects the response to *The Same Old Story*. Rame points out in her introduction to the show that coarse colloquialism in Italian is male-oriented. Terms for the male sexual organ alternate with familiar abuse of women (e.g. *figlio di puttana*, 'son of a whore') and blasphemies. English colloquialism, by contrast, is more scatological, and the frequent employment of sexual abuse is more generalised. Thus Rame's appropriation of macho language in this piece as a weapon to fight sexist attitudes loses some of its force in English when the protagonist seems simply a filthy-mouthed individual. There is nothing intrinsically shocking in such outbursts as 'Oh, you stupid prick of a dwarf, you shithead bastard, what am I going to fucking well do now?' or ' "What about this fucking wanker, then?" says the dolly': it can sound like a schoolkid's delight in using dirty language. This is not the case in the original, where the

151

woman's employment of powerfully abusive language fuels the force of her argument. It is significant that Italian – which does not have a variety of sexually abusive language – forces the scabrous dolly in the story to resort to euphemism in 'ti sbatte sul letto e cicip e ciciap . . . E anche alla mattina mette la sveglia e cicip e ciciap (*Tutta casa*, p. 79) – which in the English translation becomes 'And when he does get home he throws you on the bed and its fucketty fuck fuck fuck. Then it's fucketty fuck in the morning before you get up (*Female Parts*, 1981, p. 37).

The shock value of the language in the English translation is therefore minimalised, though the potential of the piece to disturb is in other respects very powerful. It is the cunning way in which the narrator changes her stance in order to take the audience by surprise which works so effectively. The change from her objections to the lover into acceptance of his embraces, then the way she is brutally thrown on the bed whilst continuing to be insulted, dramatises the woman's situation perfectly. The manner is which she breaks off her erotic responses – 'I talk and you listen and you talk and . . . and I . . . and I . . . ', with the change to the flat statement, 'get pregnant' (*Female Parts*, p. 28) – both re-creates the situation and comments on it. The attack on the male and his values develops from her abuse of his virility, which has a political as well as emotional force – 'Take a good look at it, go on! See? It's got a cardinal's cap on! And stripes like a general. And it's making the fascist salute. (*She raises a clenched fist.*) Yes, I did say fascist!' (ibid.) – through to her adoption of the male role in seducing the 'she-man'. Here she makes ironic use of all the blandishments her lover has employed and turns the tables on him sexually. The most powerful assault is reserved for the story to her child – one which celebrates, as in the case of Medea, the power of the woman liberated from taboos, who here is at home with the twin sides of her femininity. It is this assurance (symbolised by the melting of the dolly into her heart) which gives the force to her stand: one which is born of an awareness of how to employ her own strengths to her own ends.

The scabrous tale which concludes this monologue is characteristic of Fo at his most inspired and imaginative. It anticipates *Il fabulazzo osceno* (*Obscene Fables*) and is the episode in *Female Parts* which is closest to *Mistero buffo*. Here the actress is obliged to change her voice and manner in presenting a swift succession of characters and incidents. The stage direction in the original (inexplicably cut in the British version) makes it clear what techniques are required: *For the full duration of the story she changes position and voice according to which character she is presenting*' (*Tutta casa*, p. 77). This demands that the actress run the full gamut from the soprano squeals of the little girl to the basso profundo of the wolf, whose presence is announced by his ' "NO!" – a terrible deep voice out of the dark scary shadows of the forest'. The dwarf, the dolly, the midwife and the electronics engineer all require clear vocal characterisation, and the versatility of the performer is tested to the utmost, as she is required to maintain an ever-increasing acceleration in the shift from figure to figure. The piece as a whole has a musical structure which challenges the actress to rise to the spirited pace of the score.

Pace is the keynote of the longest of the four pieces, *A Woman Alone*. Here the bravura of the writing – which must be matched by a similar skill in performance – resides in the combination of the dramatic features of the monologue and of farce. The way in which we are gradually introduced to this woman – we listen in as she addresses a neighbour in the block opposite – both involves and alienates us. She talks of the pressure to which she, as a housewife, is subjected. Her story is a chronicle of male oppression, a deliberately exaggerated concatenation of abuses which takes familiar situations, multiplies them and assembles them into a grotesque parody which through its distortion mirrors and symbolises the position of woman in a male-dominated society. Each room of the apartment is characterised by suitably ironic music – classical music for the living-room, jazz for the kitchen, plain song for the bedroom – which is heard when the door to the room is opened. As the pace of the farce increases, so the blasts of music heard as the doors are rapidly opened and closed add to the dizzy escalation of events. This is an inspired piece, a farce for one performer. Gradually the other characters are introduced, all the more imaginatively grotesque for not appearing: the possessive husband on the other end of the phone; the peeping Tom opposite; the young boy outside the door; the heavy-breather on the phone; and the maniac brother-in-law encased in his plaster and wheelchair. The farce has a precise musical structure as the events move towards their climax and characters – like musical subjects – are introduced, reintroduced and developed. The result is a cross between Feydeau and Brecht – the Brecht of *Fear and Misery in the Third Reich* and the sketch *The Judge*, where the protagonist is obliged to cope with a variety of different problems and tensions, switching each time to a new response. Rame's monologue is a realisation of Brecht's theory of *Verfremdungseffekt*, where the actor and audience are obliged to adjust their perspective continually. The ingenuity of farce coupled with the form of the monologue challenges the versatility of the performer, who must rise to this as securely as to the verbal onslaught of *The Same Old Story*, the implacable force of *Medea* and the frantic mime of *Waking Up*. Above all, it is vital that the actress should not lose herself in the part. At the end of the piece she must be ready, shotgun in hand, calmly to take on her husband – and everything the figure stands for.

# 5
# Politics and Theatre

Non secondo me, ma secondo una concezione marxista che si rifaccia correttamente a Gramsci, la cultura dovrebbe essere la visione che si ha del mondo. L'arte, e quindi il teatro, è il modo di esprimere questo mondo. Sembra semplice, ma non è cosi. Bisogno avere ben chiaro soprattutto un punto: che la cultura è sempre in stretta relazione con il potere economico. L'intellettuale deva essere preparato per combattere accanto ai lavoratori per fare capire da dove nasce questo potere.

[It isn't my theory – it's a Marxist one, more correctly attributed to Gramsci – that culture is by definition the vision we have of the world. Art, and therefore theatre, is the way we explain this world. It seems straightforward but it isn't. You have to keep one thing absolutely clear above all: that culture is always directly related to economic power. The intellectual has to be prepared to fight alongside the workers to make the bases of this power clearly understood.]

(Dario Fo, *Spettacoli e società*, 3 Dec 1975)

In 1970, in the introduction to the Mazzotta edition of his plays, *Teatro politico di Dario Fo*: *compagni senza censura*, Fo stated,

> You always hit a problem when you talk about 'political theatre' – straightaway one thinks of Piscator's political theatre, and the term 'political theatre' employed by Piscator is a term deliberately used to provoke argument. It grew out of an opposition to the term 'alimentary theatre' and represented a type of theatre far removed from out-of-the-way problems, from dramatic and lyrical themes. Piscator's theatre was political in the crucial sense that it was directly run by the working class.   (*Compagni senza censura*, vol. 1, 1970, p. 7)

This was written at an important turning-point in Fo's theatrical career. In 1968 he and Rame had left the bourgeois theatre circuit and put themselves at the disposition of the working class by performing through the *case del popolo* – the workers' clubs administered by the ARCI, the Italian recreational and cultural association, linked very closely to the Communist Party. The style of drama they were to create in the years 1968–70 was very close to Piscator's – and Brecht's – ideal: a polemical theatre for a popular working-class audience. It is consequently relatively easy to define Fo's political position in this period.

When we look back, however, over the whole range of his work – from the early revues through the farces to the dramatic monologues, which have been the richest expression of his collaboration with Franca Rame – it is very much more difficult to pin down the centre of his political aims and achievement. Fo is not a dramatist who has developed in a logicial, inexorable way. Looking back now at his work in the late sixties, it seems remote indeed from his most recent theatrical efforts. Watching any of the plays since *Trumpets and Raspberries* – *Quasi per caso una donna, Elisabetta* (*Almost by Accident a Woman, Elizabeth*), or *Arlecchino*, for instance – one could be forgiven for believing that here is a writer with little political centre, with a minimum commitment to involve his audiences in political debate. He may seem, rather, an irresponsible satirist who takes a delight in swiping out at an indiscriminate sequence of targets. In many respects Fo appears to have returned to the period of his bourgeois theatrical writing, before the crucial change of attitude and ambience in 1968. But, then, Fo has always been first and foremost a comedian. The above passage from the introduction to the Mazzotta edition continues, significantly enough,

'When I use the term 'political theatre' now I don't want to put a lot of people's backs up. It's a natural response because political theatre has become synonymous with boring theatre, intellectual, pedantic theatre, schematised theatre, theatre that isn't any fun. (*Compagni senzo censura*, vol. 1, p. 7)

Fo's reputation is a strange one. There is a great gulf between, for instance, the political activist celebrated by the British Left in such publications as *Red Notes* and the commercial dramatist who has become, second to Ayckbourn, the bread and butter of so many West End and provincial theatres. And this difference of attitude is matched by a similar contrast of approach in Italy and abroad. Fo is regarded in Britain – and in many other countries in Europe and elsewhere – as a major contemporary dramatist. If you tell an Italian that you are interested in his work, you can be sure that the response will be surprise, based on the feeling that he is an artist who has very little to say in contemporary Italy. All this has a great deal to do with the specific political centre of Fo's work. As a popular commercial writer and performer in the decade from the late fifties to the late sixties he was at the centre of the theatrical scene. With his change of direction after 1968 he matched that of the country. The economic boom that marked the period of his great popular success was falling apart. The consumerist ethic, which rebounded on the Italian economy with a vengeance when the Japanese began to take over the market through their production of much cheaper goods in the mid sixties, was already being challenged in the student and worker movements which reached their climax in the *contestazione* of 1968. Fo was making the right decision – ethically as well as commercially – in allying himself with the forces of revolutionary change. And there is no doubt that his major productions – *Mistero buffo*, *Accidental Death of an Anarchist* and *Can't Pay? Won't Pay!* – date from this period.

But it is misleading to approach him as essentially the author of these works, plus the monologues written in collaboration with Franca Rame. For one thing, these works do not represent his current political position or explain his current reputation in Italy; for another, they do not provide a complete picture of his versatility, both in terms of dramatic skill and in his approach to ethical, social and political issues. This is not to argue that Fo is less sincere or less committed in these matters than some of his more ardent admirers outside of Italy believe. Rather, it is an attempt to see him more clearly in the context of Italian – and European – politics over the last three decades, instead of restricting him to a convenient image: as, for example, the world's leading political dramatist or a brilliant clown.

Neither of these images represents the whole truth. If we have to admit that as a political dramatist Fo has undoubtedly declined during the eighties, this is as much due to the political situation in Italy as to his own character. Fo has always been the most sensitive barometer of the political climate in his country, a shrewd critic perfectly attuned to the issues of the day. He is still that, as his devastating satire on contemporary political figures in *Arlecchino* illustrates. But the problem is that, in Italy at any rate – to use the words of Jimmy Porter – 'there just aren't any brave causes left'. As a critic of the consumerist society (which provided him with his audience) in the late fifties and the sixties, he was unequalled. And, as a more savage political critic – of state corruption, the police, economic speculation and the management of the Communist Party – in the late sixties and early seventies, he revealed a richer, more powerful side of his talent. The great issue of the seventies in Italy was terrorism: he had already written a definitive play on the subject in 1970. As a result both of the curbing of terrorism through the work of dalla Chiesa, and of the progressive decline of radical and revolutionary politics, Italy reached what has been termed *il riflusso*: ebbtide.

After the turbulent, stormy years of challenge and of rebellion, there is a less committed mood in the country. This 'couldn't care less' attitude (or *menefreghismo*, as the Italians term it) is inimical to the type of theatre Fo was producing at the end of the sixties. It is highly significant that his and Rame's drama at present is torn between two extremes: the savage onslaught of the more recent monologues written by Franca Rame (an almost desperate response to the apathy which characterises the mood of the country) and Fo's own lighter comedies. But, again, it would be short-sighted to suppose that, because these plays have very different themes and settings from Fo's dramas written in the late sixties and early seventies, they are completely lacking in political meaning and force. As Fo himself went on to say the introduction to the Mazzotta edition of his plays in 1970,

> Now we've rethought the issue: all theatre is political, all art is political; indeed precisely when the political values seem less in evidence – as in Feydeau – you have in fact the most pronounced of all political theatre, which deals with the politics of a specific social class, in this case the bourgeoisie.
>
> (*Compagni senza censura*, vol. 1, p. 7)

It is not the aim of this study to examine the whole of Fo's work. I have chosen in other chapters to highlight the most significant theatrical forms he has chosen to employ – in each case for very specific political ends. The purpose of this final chapter is to take a wider focus in order to establish the change in his political outlook as reflected in dramas at key points in his career. Again theatrical form and political content are inextricably linked and serve to reveal Fo's immense versatility. I have chosen to highlight three dramas and examine them in detail: *Gli archangeli non giocano a flipper* (*The Archangels Don't Play Pinball*, 1959), a three-act comedy composed as a sequence of revue-style sketches, which marks Fo's debut as a popular commercial dramatist; *L'operaio conosce trecento parole, il padrone mille, per questo lui è il padrone* (*The Worker Knows 300 Words, the Boss 1000*; *That's Why he's the Boss*, 1969), an epic drama with alternating episodes in contrasted styles which is the most radical piece dating from Fo's period of commitment to popular political theatre; and *Coppia aperta* (*The Open Couple*, 1983), a comedy of manners written in collaboration with Franca Rame (it supplies the first half of a programme the rest of which is made up – in stark contrast – of Rame's two powerful and disturbing monologues about a woman who has been raped and a woman who has tried to come to terms with the discovery that her son is a convicted terrorist). The three works represent Fo at three very different stages in his career and emphasise the fact that the dramatist is responding in each case to the prevailing political climate: that of the economic boom, the *contestazione* and the *riflusso*, respectively. The plays are consequently very different from each other in political content, yet they can all be properly described (following Fo) as political dramas. If we reject the political implications of revue and comedy of manners, insisting instead that the only true vehicle for the expression of political ideas is epic theatre, we blind ourselves to the diversity and complexity of political theatre – in the work of Fo or of any other dramatist.

## 'The Archangels Don't Play Pinball'

This play, with its characteristically outrageous title, was the drama which established Fo as the idol of the bourgeois theatre-going audience of the late fifties. We are in the period of *La dolce vita* – Fellini's famous comment on the hedonistic celebration of the economic boom in Italy, which had placed industrialists on the level of aristocrats and had destroyed the old social order of Italy, making glamorous actresses and pushy media individuals the gods and goddesses of a new era. Fellini, of course, was deeply critical of this new movement: his film is a classic requiem for the values of another era. But he was astute enough to realise that here was the new aristocracy. Little did he realise how soon the most sacred of all Italian values – those of individuality, of sensitivity, of genuine creativity – would be destroyed by the publicity machine that has made of the likes of Duran Duran and Wham! deities only to be compared with the latest Fiat. Fellini's comment on the sweet life seems now a mild satire, more a comment on the manners of the age. It was the era in which Fo was launched as a major dramatist, as a dramatist who, like Fellini, was intent on criticising the values of this utopia. As Fo himself has commented,

> One of the main points of departure, and in *The Archangels*, like the other works in this period, the reason for writing the play, the creative spur, came from the newspapers, from the facts which most impressed me, from the most paradoxical contradictions of the Christian Democrat state. Of course I argued my case in a way which would appeal to an audience that frequented the commercial theatre circuit. Once we'd accepted that was our audience it was obviously necessary to gear our discussion of political and social issues in that direction, hidden all the time under the cloak of satirical licence.
>
> (Valentini, *La storia di Dario Fo*, 1977, p. 64)

The play centres on the adventures of Lungo (the part

created by Fo; he could be called 'Lanky' in English), the
lad who is the butt of all the jokes his gang play on him.
And this is a drama about a group of layabouts, a gang of
youths from the *sottoproletario*, the lower fringes of the
working class, a crowd of *ragazzi di vita*, as Pasolini would
have called them. This was a new ambience for the
bourgeois drama of the period, a thrill for the wealthy
middle-class theatre-goers of Milan, newly returned from
their holidays and looking for diversion in the early part
of September, a period notoriously barren of theatrical
offerings. Fo's play inagurated a new season at the Odeon,
a theatre run by the impressario Bossino, who, having
seen Fo's previous work (in short reviews and sketches)
invited him to form a permanent company to play in his
theatre. Fo did just that: he was the author, leading actor,
director and designer; Franca Rame was the leading
actress, a soubrette, as well as administrator; two other
members of the family, Pia and Enrico, were taken into
the company along with a number of other performers,
including Piero Nuti and Mimmo Craig. The whole set-
up was very much within the tradition of the touring
company led by the *mattatore* (or actor–manager)
responsible for the programme and policy of the troupe.
The Compagnia Fo–Rame was much the same as any
other company based on nineteenth-century principles,
just such an organisation as Pirandello in the 1920s and
Strehler (more successfully) in the 1940s had attempted
to supplant with a permanent repertory company
committed to exploring the canon of major European
dramas.

Though the composition of Fo's theatre group in this
period closely resembled that of Eleonora Duse's troupe
fifty years earlier or that of Gabriele Lavia's today – an
organisation geared above all to the glorification of the

leading performer – Fo differed from other actor–
managers in that he was also a dramatist, a creative talent
of major international status. This should not, however,
blind us to the significance of the name and nature of his
theatrical organisation at this stage. The company was the
*Fo–Rame* company, and it was constituted very much
along the hierarchical lines that governed theatrical
performance in the nineteenth century. In Britain the last
such company, run by Sir Donald Wolfit, disappeared
early in the 1950s; it now seems to us a historical curiosity,
something far removed from the state-subsidised national
theatre companies dedicated to a very different programme. But the *mattatore* system, the troupe led by a
powerful actor–manager, has never really died out in Italy;
and Fo is a prime example of its continued hold. More
significantly, his own attempts, in the late sixties, to
break with this formula and found a very different,
democratically organised group met with limited success.
He is again, in the late eighties as he was in 1959, Italy's
leading *mattatore*, with his own company led triumphantly
by himself and Franca Rame.

The entrance of the gang at the beginning of *Archangels*
is a very modern image. A group of seven lads all dressed
in black trousers, braces and white shirts burst on the
scene with a catchy song glorifying their lifestyle: one of
petty theft. As they sing

> We pinch bags and radios from parked cars
> But even the cars are like pinball machines:
> Once you apply pressure, they go into tilt;
> Please, we beg you, don't do that . . .
>> (*Le commedie di Dario Fo*, vol. 1, 1966, p. 7)

We recognise an all-too-familiar Italian phenomenon. Any

foreigner who has visited Italy is bound to have been struck by the Italians' strange habit of carrying car radios around, particularly in restaurants. This is a tribute to the skill of the average Italian thief of breaking into a car and extracting the radio. Fo's play could be seen as a comment on the earliest threats to the consumerist society: one which in its sophisticated development has found a more subtle equivalent to the pilfering of car radios. A more recent development in this trendy society has been the emergence in Milan of the *paninaro*. The *paninaro* is the spoilt son of a wealthy family who finds it fashionable to eat fast food but dress in specific fashionable clothes: Timberland rough boots, a Montclair jacket and Armani jeans. The young layabouts, the eighties equivalent of Fo's gang in *Archangels*, have therefore taken to raiding the fashionable area of Milan (around Piazza San Babila) and depriving the wealthy kids of their shoes and jackets. If there seems a perverse justice in the enterprise, it is perfectly in keeping with the amoral tone of Fo's play.

Lungo is the butt of the gang's humour. They persuade him to feign stomach cramp in order to fool a baker into believing that his pastries are to blame. The idea is to force him to pay them to hush the matter up, and to get him to hand over all his cakes and buns for 'analysis'. The satire here is broad, but, when the gang hint that the baker is the victim, the real culprits being the 'big fry' who sell him the industrial substitutes blamed as the probable source of the 'poisoning', we touch on an issue which has more significant repercussions. When they go on to suggest that they take Lungo to a private clinic where the doctor – for a considerable fee – will hush up the inquiry (even if the victim should die), the satire again bites home. The gang have rigged the whole business in order to obtain the money to pay a group of prostitutes to stage a mock marriage of one of their women to Lungo, and to provide the necessary food for the ceremony. Lungo goes along with this and finds he is 'married' to the beautiful Angela. The joke over, she attempts to get rid of the whole gang, including Lungo, but finds that she – along with the gang – has bitten off more than she can chew.

Lungo is not the fool he seems. It suits his purpose to appear stupid, as he explains to her:

ANGELA (*she falls into a chair, amazed*): But what a fool you are! Not only do you realise they're making a fool of you, but you help them as well! What pleasure can you get from that?

LUNGO (*takes a cigarette out of his pocket*): No pleasure. Being taken for a ride you might say was my profession.

ANGELA: The profession of being screwed, you mean?

LUNGO: Yes. Have you heard of the *giullari*? (*He lights the cigarette.*)

ANGELA: Yes, of course I have. (*Learned, reeling it off*) The *giullari* were the people who made the kings laugh . . . right?

LUNGO (*laughing*): Absolutely right. And it's precisely the same with me. With one difference . . . since there are no longer any kings. I make my friends in the bar laugh. I'm the Rigoletto of the poor, to tell the truth . . . but the important thing is that I too earn a living by it.   (*Commedie*, vol. 1, p. 26)

This is a significant passage in the play – and in Fo's work: his first reference to the important role of the *giullare* or professional fool. It is singularly unfortunate that Tony Mitchell should have chosen this reference for the title of his book on Fo and then have called the work, perversely,

*People's Court Jester* – a perfect contradiction in terms. Verdi's Rigoletto is surely a sufficiently familiar point of reference, and we should see that Fo (via Lungo – a part he, of course, created) sees himself as fulfilling this function for the poor. There is an added significance in the Verdi reference (which would escape only a dramatic critic ignorant – as Fo is not – of the basic lyric theatrical tradition of Italy) in that Rigoletto is constrained by social and political circumstances to serve the Duke of Mantua; he is from another class and a perfect example of the clown who is seeking to break out of a situation of social and political oppression to fight the very society that is supporting him.

This is the first shock-effect in a play full of surprises. Lungo is no fool and his conversation here with Angela brings out a number of issues which have considerable satirical and political force. Lungo says to her, commenting on his height, 'I remember, for instance, when I was a boy I was so well developed that at fifteen they took me for ten years older' – to which Angela counters, 'And I remember as a girl that when I was fifteen they took me for five.' The remark puzzles Lungo until she explains that by 'five' she means '5000 lire': that is what she was paid as a child prostitute. (The Italian pun is not easy to translate. Lungo says, 'Me ne davano anche dieci', to which she retorts, 'me ne davano cinque' *Commedie*, vol. 1, p. 24). The issue of prostitution is handled directly and unromantically in the play. Critics who have complained of the sentimentality in the scenes between Lungo and Angela overlook the monetary consideration which sends Lungo away in the first act, as well as the fact that Angela's relationship with the minister later in the play is a further consequence of her social and economic role. In this first encounter between the two there is another detail – an example of Fo's brilliantly inventive visual gags – which underlines a serious point through a comic emphasis. We have seen how skilful Fo is in the later farces in using these comic gags to telling effect: they are never used as mere decoration, elaboration of the script. Here Angela tells Lungo that when she began her career she was more ignorant than she is now. 'Ignorance', she adds, 'is really the worst evil that exists. My father always said . . .' – and here she hiccups and *'repeats the phrase like a record that is stuck'* – 'my father always said . . . hic! . . . my father always said . . . '. Lungo's response is to watch her as she goes on to polish the tray she is holding as though her arm were that of a gramophone, and when he realises the nature of the problem he gently takes her arm and removes it from the tray. Her hiccups are cured.

This gag is typical of the plethora of visual jokes which run through the play. Obviously these were invented or developed in rehearsal, but the Einaudi script faithfully transcribes a large number of them. There is, for example, the gag with the chairs when the doctor calls for a seat and *'they execute a swift exchange of chairs in such a brilliant way that in the end the chairs – all six of them – go back to where they came from so that nobody manages to sit down'* (ibid., p. 10). Or the gag with the stethoscope which follows: Lungo, obeying the doctor, breathes deeply and

just as the fake doctor has placed his ear to Lungo's chest, so the first friend puts his ear to the doctor's chest, and so on – all the others repeat the action including the baker. At every cough [emitted by Lungo] the listeners react with progressive emphasis so that the effect of the sound is multiplied again and again.

(Ibid., p. 11)

169

The careful construction of the drama is particularly well illustrated by the end of Act I. Angela, having sent Lungo away and having given one of his friends short shrift when he attempts to buy her favours, changes her mind, thinking that Lungo is bound to come back to collect his coat. In fact the coat has been left by the friend, and when it is he who returns – to find Angela coyly hidden behind the screen, thinking she is talking to Lungo – he preens himself like a peacock when he hears her complimentary remarks and thinks they are meant for him. She soon relises her mistake and kicks him out, revealing her irritation by throwing the radio to the ground. It immediately gives the forecast: clear weather is expected, 'tempo sereno'. Since these two words are the real name of our hero – his surname being Tempo, his father thought it amusing to give him three different Christian names: Sereno (Clear), Nuvolo (Cloudy) and Agitato (Troubled) – Angela bursts into tears and kicks the radio across the room. The curtain is worthy of the finest well-made play.

Act II opens with a scene of cunning farce. This is Fo at his most brilliant, whilst at the same time the effect is one of cutting satire. Lungo has gone to Rome to attempt to collect the pension that is due to him for the injuries he suffered during his military service (not surprisingly, the injuries are to his coccyx or *osso sacro*, as the Italians prefer to call it). The first scene of Act II is set in a ministry in Rome; it is one which for choreographed subtlety is difficult to match in Fo's work. Lungo is presented with a series of five counters each with a shutter and, try as he will, he cannot attract the attention of a clerk behind any of them. Every time he thinks he has come to the end of the queue the shutter closes and he is obliged to try elsewhere. His own luggage – and then that of a woman trying to obtain information – gets in the way, and Fo builds up a whole ballet around the five shutters, the luggage and the other clients who arrive at exactly the wrong moment to ruin Lungo's attempt to attract the attention of one of the clerks. The height of the farce is reached as a waiter arrives carrying a tray with cups of coffee for the employees. Lungo follows him with no success to the first and second windows; he is always just too late. So, whilst the waiter is busy at the third, he moves – cunningly – to the fourth, ready and waiting. But it is not the fourth, but the fifth, shutter that opens. He has his back to this and, when he has reacted and turned, the shutter is down. 'What is the matter with the fourth one?' he asks the waiter. 'Doesn't he take coffee?' 'No', is the reply; 'he has lemon tea.' And whilst Lungo is reeling from this setback a waiter taps on the fourth shutter, it opens, he passes through the tea and leaves.

This is superb farce, but it is also an all-too-accurate presentation of the worst aspects of Italian bureaucracy. Anyone who has ever wasted an hour trying to change a traveller's cheque in any city south of Rome or has spent a whole afternoon sending a parcel abroad from Italy should take on the staff of a major bureaucratic institution, such as a ministry in Rome. I speak as one who spent three days in the Ministero degli Affari Esteri – the most daunting of buildings – trying to collect a grant. After being sent from one room to another in this temple of Fascist architecture with endless floors and endless rooms, the final torment is the fight – with some 200 other students – in the bank. The second time I undertook this challenge I was told that the problems – wasting days of students' time – had been obviated. And indeed they had. A straightforward system centring on one room and involving the simple expedient of a queue meant that 200 students were dealt with in a morning. But that did not please the bureaucracy. When I went back a month later to collect the final part of my grant I found a room full of screaming students who explained that from 8.30 that morning documents had been taken as people arrived, but nothing done. At midday, with just over an hour to go before the place closed down for the day, it was decided to allocate the grants – in reverse order of arrival. The poor individual who had got there for 8.30 was now last in the queue and there was no chance of his receiving his grant that day. The first scene of Act II in Fo's play is, for anyone who has experienced this type of bureaucratic behaviour in Italy, a masterpiece of pointed satire.

It is followed by a scene of calculated farce which matches it in subtlety. Lungo finally wins the fight in the ministry by trapping the clerks behind their shutters, pulling these down like guillotines and holding them all prisoner. He places the stamping-devices they all have round their necks on their foreheads and thus creates a sort of contraption which can process his forms efficiently. When this is fully in motion at the end of the scene it resembles, according to the stage direction, '*a Futurist machine*'. Unfortunately, the outcome of his investigations is that he has been classified as a 'hound' not as a man, as a result of the cruel games played by a past employee of the ministry, furious when he was pensioned of just before he had qualified for a substantial financial settlement. There follows a scene in the kennels in which, to avoid being put down, Lungo, who has to go through the whole process of being classified as a stray, begs a circus conjurer to take him on as a performing dog. He escapes from this ignominy onto a train, and it is there that the next witty scene of farce occurs. A minister, changing into his official clothes, has his trousers stolen by Lungo, who locks himself in the lavatory and breaks off the handle of the door when threatened by the guard. The minister, finding his trousers have gone, asks the guard for his (they are black) in return for a pair of his sporting trousers locked in his suitcase. But the key to the suitcase is in the pocket of the trousers stolen by Lungo, which initiates a wonderful farcical sequence that reaches its climax when the station master, mistaking the minister for the thief, says to him, 'It's the last time you'll play at being a minister, my lad!' – to which the bewildered official replies, 'I'm finished as a minister? What are you saying? Has the government been overthrown – *again*?' (*Commedie*, vol. 1, p. 69).

In the last act Lungo plays out his role as minister – a minister who gains great popularity by performing the conjuring-tricks he has learnt in his earlier life – and is finally reunited with Angela. The significance of the title is seen towards the end of the play in a scene which resolves the Pirandellian implications of the plot throughout. Fo makes it clear that the play is written for twelve actors who carefully double up a number of parts. Considerable humour is extracted throughout the play from the fact that characters reappear in different disguises, to the consternation of Lungo. When in Act III scene ii we return to the situation at the end of the first scene of the play, it becomes clear that all the crazy events – the transformation of the hero into a dog and the obsessive recurrence of the characters in different roles – has been a dream. Lungo is heartbroken, because this implies that his relationship with Angela was also imagined. But his friends proceed to take him through the wedding service-again – except that this time, in the tradition of fairy stories, his bride is ugly. He rails against the archangels, saying they have rigged everything and that they play with human beings as with pinball machines, sending them all too readily into tilt. But his amusing travesty of Gloucester's 'As flies to wanton boys are we to the gods./They kill us for their sport' (*King Lear*) is tempered by the fact that Angela removes her wig and glasses to reveal the beauty he fell in love with. Moreover, the money he had obtained in the dream is also real, so that the two of them can begin a life together.

This play – a strange mixture of revue sketches, farce, Pirandellian theatrical games and political satire – is an important and attractive work from Fo's earlier career. It was written to amuse, and there is no doubt that its brilliant inventiveness is irresistible. Moreover, it represents that side of Dario Fo – 'the jester of the bourgeoisie' – which in Britain at any rate has tended to be relegated to the annals of history, overshadowed by his more obviously politically oriented drama. Unless we respect, however, the political dramatist in the earlier plays, it is impossible to understand the true nature and versatility of Fo the dramatic critic.

### 'The Worker Knows 300 Words, the Boss 1000; That's Why he's the Boss'

This drama is one of the most original, fascinating and underestimated of Fo's works. It is one of the plays written during that period of committed political activism (1968– 70) when Fo and Rame had abandoned their own theatrical company and were working instead through the Associazione Nuova Scena. The play was written to be performed in the *case del popolo* (the working people's clubs) in the north-west of Italy, and Fo went so far as to set the play in just such a building. Rame has explained the significance of this:

The workers' social clubs (*case del popolo*) in Italy represent a peculiar and very widespread phenomenon. They were set up by workers and peasants at the turn of the century, when the first socialist cells began to appear. The fronts of these first buildings used to bear the following inscription: 'If you want to give to the poor, give five coppers, two for bread and three for culture', and culture does not only mean being able to read and write, but also to express one's own creativity on the basis of one's own world view.

(*Can't Pay? Won't Pay!*, 1982, p. vii)

What precisely had brought these two performers to work in such venues instead of on the conventional theatre circuit? In the first place, their plays were stirring up more and more polemic and were bringing them into conflict with the law and the censor. From the start their work had always aroused a strong measure of antagonism from the conservative Right, and in 1963 they had stopped working in television when their satirical review *Canzonissima* was subjected to heavy censorship. In 1967 their savage attack on American imperialism *La signora e da buttare* (*The Woman Should be Kicked Out*) – in which 'La signora' is a personification of America – had met with a mixed reception on the commercial circuit. More significantly, Fo was summoned and threatened with arrest for comments 'offensive to a foreign head of state', comments (on President Johnson) that had in fact been improvised and therefore had not been approved initially by the censor. This incident worked against Fo and Rame when they tried (unsuccessfully) to obtain visas to visit the United States. Ever acutely sensitive to the political atmosphere, Fo was gradually moving towards the adoption of a stance in direct opposition to the establishment. In this respect he was influenced by the growing solidarity of workers and students, which found its strongest expression in the summer of 1968. In the spring of that year, students in Paris, themselves influenced by the earlier campus riots in America (at Berkeley and then elsewhere), had set out to fight the system with revolution. The idea spread. The theatre itself was going through a radical new phase of rethinking its role. Giorgio Strehler had broken with the Piccolo Teatro in the same year to form his own troupe dedicated to more overtly political work. In France, Barrault, dismissed from the Odéon for his support of the revolutionary student committee, formed his own new company. Even in Britain – the one European country largely untouched by the upheaval that was taking place elsewhere – Peter Brook, in 1967, had produced *US* with the Royal Shakespeare Company: a documentary attack on the American involvement in Vietnam.

In this context it is important to consider Fo's own standpoint:

What I had been trying to do for some years was to make my audiences aware of the true dimension of power, to take the mask off its appearance. Let me point out after all that revolution is scarcely born because somebody wakens up one morning and says, 'What a lovely day. Let's create the revolution.' It's a question of patiently working towards an end – for a long period, maybe for decades. It's a question of learning how to steer people's rage. Of starting to propose to people a different vision of the world, on the cultural level as well. In other words to create in people first and foremost the awareness of being exploited, and to make them see the extent of that exploitation. Of getting the worker to say not merely, 'My god, the boss is taking my money from me', but to show him that there's exploitation in the fact that they steal your language, your proverbs, your way of singing. That they disguise your history, tell you a load of nonsense about how you were born, about the real significance of every revolution. That they even make you move when you go out dancing within exactly the same space in which you move at the factory, on the production line. That indeed they force you to make love with the very words they put into your mouth.   (Valentini, *La storia di Dario Fo*, pp. 8–9)

This statement of Fo's political stand, from a long interview with Chiara Valentini published in the magazine *Panorama* in 1973 (and entitled, significantly, 'Il rompiscatole' – 'The Shit Stirrer'), finds powerful echoes in *The Worker*. This is a drama concerned with the very question of the theatre's role in the revolutionary process of educating the worker, making him aware of his history and culture so that he is better equipped to fight the system. The play was not liked: this time, however, not by the cultural establishment (who didn't see it), but by the conservative wing of the Communist Party itself. Fo and Rame had deliberately set themselves the task of revaluing the role of the party within the revolutionary context of the late sixties. The play's setting – in the disused library of a *casa del popolo* – is the perfect metaphor for the betrayal of that social and political purpose for which the clubs were originally founded, a betrayal for which the party is held responsible. As Rame went on to explain in her discussion of the role of the workers' clubs,

However, by working in these places, we realised that
the original need to study and produce culture together,
which inspired workers and peasants to build their own
clubs, had been completely dissipated. The clubs had
become nothing more than shops, selling more or less
alcoholic drinks, or dance halls or billiard rooms . . .
The working-class parties had failed to follow up the
needs for creative expression that had been manifested
so powerfully among workers and peasants. This failure
was based on their persuasion that it is useless to
stimulate the development of a proletarian culture, since
this does not and cannot exist.

(*Can't Pay? Won't Pay!*, pp. vii–viii)

As *The Worker* opens, we find ourselves in a dusty
library where a group of men and women are busily
dismantling the shelves and stacking the books away in
boxes to make way for billiard tables. The library is to be
a games room. Here Fo has hit on a spectacular central
image – which he manipulates and develops throughout
the play with immense skill – to present the corrosion of
cultural values and the party's neglect of its duty. As
Angela had pointed out in *Archangels*, 'Ignorance is really
the worst evil that exists': what the workers are being
denied here is the access to their own history, their own
culture. It is not just a matter of being denied theatre,
though the theatre is arguably the most social and political
form of artistic communication. There is more to Fo's
concern than that very genuinely expressed by Wilfred
Harrison, director of the Bolton Octagon Theatre, when,
as we were driving through Sheffield in 1984, he pointed
with absolute contempt to the publicity of the Crucible
Theatre proudly proclaiming it 'the home of television
snooker'. In the course of the play Fo's workers literally

dip into their culture, open books, with the result that ideas, characters, events leap at them, are brought to life before their eyes. Thus they learn a great deal about themselves through their history – they learn about things they were ignorant of: they are permitted to see things banned (by their own party, as keen as their economic oppressors to stifle what is potentially dangerous) – and through this they learn to question, to argue, to reason. At the end of the play, as they reassemble the books on the shelves, they are active participants in the reclamation of their own culture.

As the workers begin to clear the library they rehearse all the prejudices against reading and book-learning: television has destroyed the habit; books are hard work, full of long incomprehensible words; culture is for the rich. Fo cunningly anticipates all the prejudices his own audience are likely to share. But then he begins to insert a series of ideas which make it clear that the situation is not so simple. One of the workers reads a passage from one of the books she's clearing: 'a man without culture is like an empty sack: very impressive when filled with wind, but when it rains – and it often rains on the revolution – you find the sack screwed up under your feet and you trip over it' (*Le commedie di Dario Fo*, vol. 3, 1975, p. 86). The metaphor – it is a quotation from Mao Tse-tung – is powerful and has an effect. So does the argument of one of the other, wittier colleagues when a copy of the gospels is discovered among the books, and he argues that this is the story of a political assassination, of somebody who for ever criticised the rich. When asked what should be done with the copy, he is told it ought to be placed on the Vatican's Index of banned books. The Fo of *Mistero buffo* is very much in evidence.

The way in which Fo really begins to interest his

audience and involve them in political discussion is through his unparalleled narrative gifts. Suddenly, as the workers are arguing, one of them shouts, 'No, I won't allow you to insult me . . . I never betrayed anyone . . . you know that better than I do.' She is quoting from a book about Stalinist trials in Czechoslovakia, employing the words of Bornia Kvanic, who was accused by the regime of Trotskyite sympathies. As a simple lighting-change takes place, the character himself steps out of one of the very boxes into which the books are being packed and his trial is re-enacted before us. Thanks to Fo's subtle irony, it is no straightforward issue, and he gradually and carefully involves his audience not merely in a historical event but also in the dialectic which arises from it. As Kvanic is interrogated by a people's commissar for his supposed betrayal of Communism during the Spanish Civil War, another commissar springs to life – this time one of Franco's henchmen. The irony, as Kvanic recalls the torture he underwent in Spain for his Communist sympathies, is telling, the more so as the two interrogators vie with one another to extract the truth from their prisoner, Franco's commissar at one point pushing his rival aside when he claims that he was first: 'No. Not chronologically the first. If you don't mind, the Spanish Civil War came a bit earlier!' (*Commedie*, vol. 3, p. 90).

This type of wit does not appeal to one of the workers, described as a 'Stalinist', nor does the dramatisation of events which follows. Here Fo enters in detail, via his character Kvanic, into a reconstruction of the trial of one of the main Czech leaders, Slansky. Fo's narrative is based on the autobiography of Slansky's widow, Josepha – *Report on my Husband*, published in both Italy and Britain in 1969. Fo's character Kvanic, significantly enough, is an invention, a dramatic device to draw his audience into the story. There is a powerful theatrical and emotional tension between the condemned Kvanic and his wife when she visits him in prison. She recalls her first meeting with him, after he had been released from Dachau, but tells him that she must now reject him as the party says he is guilty of treason. Together they recall and re-enact one of the most stirring incidents of the war: their struggle over snow-covered mountains during a blizzard in an attempt to evade the Germans. One of their party, Sverma, wounded and weak, falls back, but Slansky insists they go to find him and rescue him. At this point a judge appears and Fo initiates a telling counterpoint between the trial of Slansky and his heroic action in the war. The actor playing Slansky is required to cut effortlessly between the two scenes, acted simultaneously to stunning epic theatrical effect. As he lifts Sverma on his shoulders and incites his comrades to sing a stirring revolutionary hymn, Slansky reels off a series of admissions of guilt, of betraying his country and of being directly responsible for the death of Sverma. This disturbs Marta, Kvanic's wife, as she watches this dual re-creation of history. It seems that Slansky is reciting a series of charges which are plainly denied by his actions. That is just the point. Fo illustrates how the Stalinist trials were rigged and emphasises – through the most straightforward, yet telling, dramatic devices – how important it is to study our history carefully, research it, and refuse to accept simplisitic truths. Marta finally realises that Slansky's trial was 'a farce written by policemen'. We have witnessed the destruction of a loyal and courageous genius who refused to play the game according to the rules made by party bureaucrats, who then set about systematically rewriting his story for posterity.

The drama continues without interruption (the interval indicated in the Einaudi edition is misleading) as further

scenes in sharp contrast are brought to life. We move now
to a factory floor and the discussion of a group of workers
with a young intellectual who has joined the staff. They
reel off all their prejudices against him – mocking him for
his trendy glasses and delicate hands, and labelling him a
*terrone* (someone from the south and therefore ignorant) –
but they find it more and more difficult to resist the logic
of his arguments. He is no airy-fairy intellectual but a
practical man intent on convincing his fellow workers of
the extent to which they are being continually exploited.
The 'improvements' in working conditions are only a
means to a greater productivity: if their work is no longer
backbreaking, it puts far more strain on their eyes. 'Ours
is a party directed by intellectuals. The workers must
become the intellectuals of the party', he argues and states,
'The worker knows, because he represents the vanguard
of the revolution, because the people have a great culture.
The power of the bourgeoisie, the aristocracy and the
Church has in large measure destroyed it, buried it, but it
is our duty to see that it is recovered (*Commedie*, vol. 3,
p. 107). This is pure Gramscian Marxism and it comes as
a theatrical shock to discover, during the course of the
scene, that this is in fact Gramsci himself speaking. In his
conversations with workers in Turin in the early twenties
he sowed the seeds of modern Italian Communism. In his
later notebooks written in prison he provided the basis
for a revolutionary Marxism which challenged the
intellectual to discover the people's culture and help to
reanimate it. This challenge was taken up very forcefully
in the late sixties both by theatre practitioners such as Fo
and by academics. This was the real nature of the
revolution within European universities in that period,
and its marked influence is widely felt today. But putting
Gramsci on stage in this play Fo pays tribute to the

philosopher whose ideas fuelled his own political theatre, and at the same time illustrates Gramsci's technique in practice.

The Gramscian discussion is interrupted by the sounds of a guitar: a musician is playing a few snatches of the ballad of Michele Lu Lanzone, and as he is questioned closer about the story it is re-enacted for us. An old woman comes on stage carrying a rag doll. As she sings along with the musician she plays with her own hair, combs the doll's and cradles the doll as though it were a small child. We have begun the play's *pièce de resistance*: a long and emotional monologue narrating the tragic struggle of the Sicilian poor against the power of the Mafia. The ballad is a particularly telling theatrical and musical form: it is popular, simple, straightforward in narrative and emotionally charged. The Einaudi edition instructs the actress to perform this scene '*with no reference to naturalism; in the epic style*'. This is crucial, since the events of the story and the situation of the woman – we realise at the start that she is mentally deeply disturbed, and discover later that she is in an asylum – contain intense emotional potential. The actress must in no sense be carried away by emotional involvement in the role, and the audience at the end must be left to think through the implications of the story, which is overwhelming in its tragic intensity.

It is the story of the mother of Michele Lu Lanzone, a union leader who set himself against the bosses and the Mafia system. For some strange reason Tony Mitchell insists on calling her the wife. This is a grave misunderstanding of the story, to say nothing of the fact that it misses the point of Fo's careful contrast between the three major female roles in the play: a wife, a mother and a mistress (their emotional and social significance being carefully thought through). Fo has constructed the monologue in such a way that it is virtually impossible to play the part with a Stanislavskian sense of identification. The actress is required to play all the characters in the story, to switch from one to another rapidly – notably from the mother (with her desperate wish to protect her son) to Michele (with his impetuous and outspoken conduct). The actress is also given very clear points of focus which force her to externalise and not internalise her performance. She talks frequently to the doll (her last vestige of contact with her son), to the guitarist and to the audience. The switches between different emotional registers – pleading, authoritative, furious, exultant, murderous, and so on – are charted with the precision of a vocal score.

By contrast the story itself is a horrific one. Describing how Michele insisted on presenting the people's case to the authorities, the mother tells how he and his followers were beaten and imprisoned. This did not stop him. He found an old map with the source of a stream marked. Aware that the discovery of this would free the people from their dependence on the landlords because it would give them a free water supply, he pledged himself to discover the blocked source. The story alternates between the mother's warnings and his refusal to turn back, describing the jubilant atmosphere when the source was found (with the people bathing and dancing in the water) and later the terrible reason why the water supply suddenly dried up: Michele had been killed by the Mafia and his body used as a cork to bung up the source. After the mother has spoken of Michele's imprisonment the action is interrupted by the entry of two nurses who discuss the *strozzina*, a primitive way of quietening down patients by smothering them in a wet sheet until they pass out through asphyxiation. In a sense we are therefore prepared for them to inflict this on the mother at the end of her story as she loses all control and calls on the lava of the volcano to devour the men who have killed her son and yet have escaped justice. As the mother faints, the nurses calmly straighten out the sheet and hold it there, using it as a curtain behind which the actress makes her exit. The complete control of the emotive charge of political drama is here in evidence, concentrated into a *tour de force* for the solo actress which was to prove a seminal point for the later development of Fo and Rame's theatre.

We are not allowed to dwell too long on the tragic implications of this story, as a gun-shot is heard and one of the actors falls down, apparently dead. We soon learn this is Mayakovsky, the revolutionary Soviet playwright, and the final section of the play is – in very sharp contrast to the monologue – a comic, ironic presentation of his death, culminating in a re-creation of one of his satirical dance dramas. Irony underpins the whole investigation into Mayakovsky's suicide as Fo sets out to debunk the conventional party line that it was the gesture of an extravagant and spoilt artist. Again – as with the Stalinist in the Czech scenes – the police agent is deaf to irony. As one of the actresses (Fo's, not Mayakovsky's) points out that they had been talking to 'this chap who was Gramsci just before' the suspicions of the police officer are aroused: 'Who is this Gramsci?' he wants to know; 'Friend of the deceased? . . . What was he talking about? Politics? . . . Whose side was he on?' (*Commedie*, vol. 3, p. 116). Fo's delight in joking with the theatrical medium – a feature which places him firmly in the tradition of Goldoni and Pirandello – is here used to condemn the soulless bureaucrats who would stifle his own imagination. This scene is followed by one with the Minister of Culture, who sheds crocodile tears over the death of Mayakovsky. The figure is a splendid Fo caricature of the self-important bureaucratic figure, who could equally have come from the cast of one of Mayakovsky's own plays. He argues with Anna Janaceskaja (Mayakovsky's mistress and leading actress) over the fate of the dramatist and she informs him of the poet's final plans before his death.

With a clear reference to the vicissitudes suffered by Fo's drama in Italy, Anna points out that it is the public, not a group of bureaucratic censors, who should judge the worth of a dramatist. The Minister of Culture is outraged, saying that this is only her opinion. 'No,' she counters, 'it's Lenin's!' and goes on to argue for the freedom of the artist. When the Minister argues that she is asking for anarchy, pure and simple, she counters, 'in fact that's exactly what Lenin said. "In art we see anarchy in the most fundamental sense of the word imaginable" ' (ibid., p. 120). The Minister cannot answer this: she has made her point as clearly as Fo has in stating through this parallel his clear Marxist–Leninist stand. The bureaucrats of his own party were already proving as insensitive and destructive as those who had silenced Mayakovsky. Anna now takes the opportunity to present her 'Futurist ballet', in which Fo utilises a technique of Mayakovsky to present – in mime and dance – a satirical view of the political situation in the late sixties. Amongst his targets are the Communist mayor of Bologna flirting with a right-wing cardinal, the Americans terrorising the Vietnamese, and the political opportunism of several Eastern-bloc countries.

The play ends with a further parallel between Fo's theatrical activity and that of his mentor. We are shown how Mayakovsky too, rejected by the theatre establishment, took to presenting his shows in factories.

As Anna recalls this, one of the most celebrated of his performances is re-created: the occasion on which Mayakovsky was asked to recite his own poem on the death of Lenin, and as he did so the audience joined in to overwhelming effect. An alternation between solo voices and powerful choric expression accompanies the rebuilding of the shelves as the books are put back, and is carried over into the final utterances of the drama as the workers recapitulate the major themes of the play: the quotations from Mao and Gramsci, the Czech partisan song, even the motto over the *casa del popolo*. In a forceful theatrical *gestus*, vital living proof is offered of the ability, through determination and education, to rediscover and reconstruct the workers' culture.

Unfortunately, this was not how the Communist Party – or, at least, those members whose voices were most powerfully heard – saw it. Though the original *Unità* critic liked the show, his notice was withdrawn and replaced by a review by an unnamed critic who accused Fo, Rame and their company of 'a coarse sentimental lack of political muscle which is an offence to objective reporting and which distorts the facts'. The cultural representative for the ARCI circuit, Pagliarini, came to see the show and organised a discussion after the performance at the Ariston cinema in Sestri Levante in which he accused the actors of putting on a show the aim of which was not to help the oppressed but to change the structure of the party. Rame, incensed by his attitude and the way the discussion was going, seized the microphone and announced through sobs, 'you are the people and the audience who are guaranteed to wreck any attempt to establish an alternative theatre circuit'. It was clear that Fo and Rame, influenced by the revolutionary spirit in the air, were setting themselves firmly against the conventional party line.

Shortly afterwards, with the Piazza Fontana bombing in Milan (the incident which was to provide Fo with the material for his most disturbingly effective play, *Accidental Death of an Anarchist*), the split between the company and the party became more marked, as the company took a radical political stand and the party withdrew into a more conservative position, dissociating itself from any activity which related to terrorism.

But the problem for Fo and Rame was more complex. It had to do with theatrical as well as practical politics. Whereas in *Archangels*, for example, Fo had written a drama around a lead actor, a soubrette and a supporting cast, in *The Worker* he had attempted to construct a play for a group of dedicated political performers who had no relationship whatsoever with the old hierarchical system of the stage. The play is written, quite simply, for a group of twelve actors who cover some thirty roles. This is very different from the doubling in *Archangels*, where the roles of Lungo and Angela are outside this system and the rest of the cast provide a chorus. *The Worker* is conceived as a piece for a group of actors with no stars or supporting players. This was not how it turned out. In the end Franca Rame played all three of the major female characters: Marta Kvanic, the mother of Michele Lu Lanzone and Anna Janevskaja. The same situation as had arisen in their first play for the new group, *Grande pantomima con bandiere e pupazzi piccoli e medi* (*Big spectacular with flags and small and medium puppets*), was repeated, as Fo himself relates:

> We were hankering after a utopian situation, because when you abolish one system it's necessary to substitute another. To be fair we weren't on an equal footing. Particularly when it came to performing on stage, we

188

could only pretend to be equals. There were professional actors such as Franca and I, and others who were plainly amateurs. So that in the name of egalitarianism and the destruction of the concept of the star we gave ourselves a sort of handicap, played down our parts so as not to put the others in the shade. In *Grande pantomima*, for instance, Franca and I had chosen to play very small supporting roles. However, when we put the show into production everybody realised that when we weren't on stage the action ground to a halt. So we were forced to change the pace, invent fresh gags. When the show was ready for performance it was we two who yet again had the leading roles. There were protests; we were accused of manipulating the issue.

(Valentini, *La storia di Dario Fo*, p. 106)

### 'The Open Couple'

Fo and Rame were not made to be supporting actors in a theatrical commune. They are by nature and training stars, *mattatori*, and to deny this is to hamper and destroy their effectiveness both as actors and as political commentators. It is therefore no surprise to find them returning in the early seventies to a style of drama which gave precedence to their particular skills. After the events of the late sixties their theatre could never be the same again: Franca Rame had gained a political awareness and confidence from the revolutionary movement which meant that she saw her own role as a woman and as an actress in a completely different light. And both of them had become fully aware of the need to continue the political fight via the alternative theatrical circuit. *Accidental Death of an Anarchist* – the play Fo created immediately after breaking with the ARCI network and founding a theatrical *collective* called La Comune (in sharp contrast to both the '*Organizzazione* Nuova Scena' and the '*Compagnia* Fo–Rame') – is his most compelling work, since he found in it both the subject matter and the dramatic form best suited to extend his talents as a political satirist. One of the major problems he and his company have faced since their break with the official party system has been the lack of a base. The occupation of the Palazzina Liberty in Milan from 1974 until the early eighties provided some form of venue, however unsatisfactory; but his nomadic existence in recent years – playing in unsatisfactory venues from converted cinemas to outmoded theatres – has thrown him too persistently on his own resources with the result that his utopian plans for a popular political theatre have been compromised by the constant need to attract fresh audiences. The result is that, in certain crucial respects, he has returned to an old-fashioned mode of theatre which at times too closely resembles the professional set-up he so firmly rejected in the late sixties.

Nothing could be further from the content and styles of the dramas written in the Nuova Scena period than the comedy of manners, *The Open Couple*. The full Italian title is in fact, *Coppia aperta – quasi spalancata*, which could be translated into English as *The (Wide) Open Couple*. The Italian language does not lend itself easily to word-play and it is therefore all the more striking that so many of the jokes in this play are verbal. The staging-techniques employed in the drama are no less witty. It opens with the husband shouting outside the bathroom door in a desperate attempt to get his wife to come out. As the lights come up on another side of the stage, the actress steps forward to announce, 'The irresponsible maniac locked in the other room – that is the bathroom –

is me. The other person, the one who's shouting at me and begging me not to be so bloody stupid is my husband' (*Coppia aperta*, 1984, p. 7). Fo had used the same ploy in *Trumpets and Raspberries*, but in the later drama the potential of the theatrical device is carried much further. From the start the convention of the theatrical 'fourth wall' is broken down: the presence of the audience is constantly acknowledged throughout the play. Indeed, the husband and wife of Fo's domestic comedy use the audience in much the same way as George and Martha have recourse to Nick and Honey in Albee's *Whose Afraid of Virginia Woolf*?

This Pirandellian joking with the conventions of the dramatic medium gives rise to several very telling moments, such as that early in the play when the wife attempts to commit suicide by jumping out of the window:

> WOMAN *makes to go in front of the window. The husband who is pressed against the window, stops her.*
> MAN: Look out! There's a sheer drop there!
> WOMAN: No, there's the stage.
> MAN: Yes, but the set finishes here.
> WOMAN: Yes, but I'm in an imaginary world. I'm telling my version of the story now, so I'm coming out of character; that means I can come out of the set as well . . . (*Coppia aperta*, p. 8)

A little later, when the woman promises not to shoot herself, the husband relaxes, only to find she threatens to shoot him instead. She fires at him and narrowly misses. 'I'm not included in the theatrical fiction, then?' he comments. 'Of course not!' is her response as she pushes home her advantage at gun-point. The play is a brilliant dramatisation of the power struggle between two highly articulate middle-class people which is psychologically accurate while aware of the familiar emotional clichés, which it mocks with considerable relish. There is a ridiculing of the fashionable existential *Angst* of the male partner, who – when his wife takes a leaf out of his own book and finds herself a lover – wants the woman he knew (or thought he knew) back at all cost: a scene which parodies Pirandello, and such late dramas as *Trovarsi* (which I translated for the BBC as *A Woman in Search of Herself*) in particular.

> MAN: I seem to have become . . . I don't know how to put it . . . that's it, a complete stranger, as though I were in another world . . . I want you as you were before, my God, please try to find yourself again . . . that same woman who will insult me . . . talk dirty . . . want to jump out of the window . . . shoot me . . . without possessing me. This is the Antonia I prefer . . . Find yourself again!
>
> WOMAN: Find myself again? Whatever are you saying that for? What drivel! It has all the profundity of old chocolate wrappings! What the hell does 'find yourself' mean? 'The real me'? 'No, I'm not going out today . . . I haven't discovered myself yet!' 'Sorry about the delay, but I haven't found myself yet!!' 'Who's been mucking about with my ego? Good god, it was here a minute ago!' 'Excuse me, sir, have you seen "my real self" by any chance?' 'Yes, it was riding a bicycle with your Oedipus complex on the handlebars!' (*Coppia aperta*, p. 17)

The drama mercilessly pillories these clichés of bourgeois psychological theatre because, though it is concerned with a very precisely observed relationship in a middle-class setting, its aim is entirely political. It is not merely that Fo and Rame are examining sexual politics in the play – though that is an important part of their aim: the psychological conflict throughout is seen in relation to the social and political implications of the couple's lifestyle.

For example, when the wife first discovers her husband's infidelities, he blames the whole thing on the political situation: the *riflusso*, the defeat of the revolutionary movement, the collapse of political ideals. These, he insists, are realities – to which her response is 'Fair enough, somebody who is disillusioned politically throws himself into the Hari Krishna movement . . . opens a macrobiotic restaurant . . . or opens his own personal brothel!' The boot is very firmly on one foot in the earlier part of the play, as the promiscuity is entirely that of the husband; therefore, of course, the satire favours the wife's point of view. After a particularly vivid and amusing passage in which the wife relates her impression of the husband collecting women like so many rare mushrooms, and her obsessive picturing of them transformed into mice in the wardrobe, in the soapdish, in her shoes, the husband retorts with the accusation that, 'just for the sheer pleasure of gratifying three or four of your fanatical ball-breaking feminist friends, you're really determined to lynch me'.

The wife's attempts to get her own back on her husband are given particularly sharp theatrical focus in the play. For example, when he returns on one occasion and asks her to help him with his latest (young) girlfriend, the whole scene is re-enacted with switches from direct speech to commentary, with very amusing consequences:

WOMAN (to the audience): One day my husband came to me, all embarrassed and asked,

MAN: Listen, these women's matters . . . why don't you
go with Piera . . .

WOMAN: Piera was the girl's name . . .

MAN: . . . to the gynaecologist to get her fitted with a
coil. Perhaps you can succeed in convincing her. She'll
go along with you for certain.

WIFE: I was being asked to act the mother with Pierina
. . . sure . . . I'll go along with her to the
gynaecologist: 'Excuse me, sir, would you be so kind
as to fit my husband's fiancée with the coil.' Let's
hope he shares our sense of humour. I'll fit you
with the coil . . . up your nose, one end up each
nostril! (Ibid., pp. 10–11)

Later, when the wife has discovered a lover – thanks to
the encouragement of their son, who, very much the child
of this trendy couple of the 1960s, tells his mother he is
fed up with the arguments and bad atmosphere at home
and persuades her to take a leaf out of his father's book
(provided he's younger than her husband and not a
socialist) – her revelation of all this to her husband is again
acted out whilst they are having a quiet game of cards.
The husband's response – to the fact of her own infidelity,
and to the revelation that the lover is a brilliant young
academic who has considerable fame as a pop singer – is
physicalised (through his dropping of the cards and
attempts to shuffle them) to great comic effect.

But the play is very fair on the issue of the male–female
war game enacted. The wife's lover is rather too good to
be true – a somewhat exaggerated vendetta on her part –
and he, along with the wife, is subjected to the ironic
scrutiny of Fo and Rame. The husband is delighted,
for instance, that the wife has experienced considerable
difficulty in actually sleeping with the 'egg-head', and their

first failure (in a hotel bedroom) is described in such a way as to make fun of both of them. Moreover, their trendy determination to join a group of protesters heading for the nuclear base at Comiso, in Sicily (the Italian equivalent of Greenham Common), and their inability to do so (they stop off at Parma and find the city so attractive that they stay there) places their political commitment in a suitably ironic context. They have taken off to Sicily (from Milan) not by plane, not by car, but on the lecturer's (old) motorbike, which is a further source of vengeful hilarity to the husband – and to the audience. But this issue of a sexual vendetta is analysed still further as the husband admits that he is wallowing in 'the fat sugary pleasure of the reactionary' when he discovers to his delight that the 'egg-head' has a daughter who is a drug addict. Indeed, this is how the wife and he have met, as the result of her determination to involve herself in useful social work to forget her husband's infidelities. It serves to bring the ironic wheel full circle.

This highly entertaining – often savage – comedy of sexual manners, a political as well as an emotional struggle, formed the first half of a double bill which had a radical change of tone after the interval. The comedy has been performed in Britain as a fringe lunchtime show, and as such proved to have as little bite as a revival of a Coward play. The audience for the British fringe has little taste for this style of theatre. What they would have made of the second part had it been performed is another matter altogether, since this consisted of two monologues by Franca Rame, very hard-hitting emotionally and striking at very clear political issues. The first is the account of a rape, taken from the magazine *Quotidiano donna* but clearly influenced by Rame's own experience at the hands of fascist thugs in March 1973. In a sense this represents

195

the perfect example of 'emotion recollected in tranquillity'. Perhaps 'tranquillity' is the wrong word, but the passing of time and the recognition of the similar experiences of other women has given Rame the power to evoke this experience in crystal-clear narrative terms which are far more effective than an emotive description of the event could ever be. The other monologue – a much longer one – narrates with consummate skill the no-less-traumatic experiences of a mother who has found out that her son is a convicted terrorist and who describes the humiliations she has undergone in an attempt to visit him in prison.

*The Rape* (*Lo stupro*) has a crucial introduction by Rame in which she emphasises the iniquity of the Italian legal system, which makes it particularly difficult to report such a crime. Every pressure is put on the victim by the judge and the defending counsel to admit that she incited the rape or took some pleasure in it. The specific questions asked in court are outlined in all their obscene detail. The narrative then follows. It is enacted by Rame either seated or standing, depending on the auditorium, but without moving or resorting to any form of physical emphasis. She relates the incident in a sort of abbreviated narrative not dissimilar to a television account of the facts. Brechtian epic theatre could go no further. The incident, however, is recalled with a number of sharp, telling visual references which, whilst they give an impression of the particular situation of the victim, in no way add a subjective emotional gloss. The woman recalls the music playing on the radio the men had with them; she remembers being held from behind by one of them in a way that makes her think of how children used to have teeth extracted before the age of anaesthetics. This visual metaphor is particularly strong: she goes on to describe how she concentrated on other issues in an attempt to block out the painful reality of the situation – much as one does in the dentist's chair. The most degrading and frightening element of the experience was when she realised that the men intended not merely to rape her, but to torture her as well. This too is described without any attempt to arouse emotion – as a fact which slowly dawned on her as they began to use their cigarettes to burn her. In the session at Riverside Studios in May 1983 when Franca Rame worked on the piece with British performers she underlined this moment – this change of intensity in the narration – as crucial. The monologue ends with the woman outside the police station. The most terrible irony of all is that she is almost as afraid of the police as she was of the men who violated her. Hence she resolves to put off the reporting of the crime.

One of the most effective features of the narrative style of this monologue is the careful control of the time-scale. Though the account ends with the avoidance of a confession to the police, it is clear from other references within the monologue that we are dealing not merely with a personal account of a disturbing event but with a carefully documented case history. She recalls the immediate facts of her cardigan and other clothes being torn off with a knife. She recalls the sensation when her skin was cut. But that particular paragraph ends with the comment, 'The medical investigation revealed that the cuts were twenty centimetres long.' This ability to step out of the narrative and make us aware that we are at the same time dealing with a precisely reconstructed crime is one of the most skilful features of both these monologues.

The careful control of the time factor in *The Mother* (*La madre*) is what gives the story its force – both as a powerfully gripping narrative and as an objective political commentary on the events. The account is carefully divided into a number of episodes: eleven in all. The story is a complex one, since Rame has set herself the challenging task not merely of bringing to life the torment of this mother, but also of explaining it: of telling us why these things have come about and what steps we, as an audience, might take to remedy the situation. This is in the fullest sense of the phrase what the critic Renzo Sanson has described as 'militant theatre'.

The opening section grabs the audience directly as Rame asks her listeners to imagine themselves in a situation whereby they saw on the television screen a picture of their own son as a convicted terrorist. What would their response be? As she describes her own experience she jumps back in time in an attempt to work out why her son has come to this. A sequence of four sections looks back over her son's childhood: he was brought up according to the most modern theories of child-training. (It is perhaps worth interjecting here that, if Italian children were not given all the privileges of adults – in the extreme way in which they are indulged in public – with none of their responsibilities, it is possible that fewer of them would grow up into the childish monsters they so often become.) The mother recalls the crucial events of the late sixties and contrasts the apparent clarity of the political issues – the heroes such as Che Guevara, and the villains such as the Americans in Vietnam – with the more complex nature of the political situation which has developed since.

What emerges from the mother's account as the main reason for her son's conduct is his disillusion and his bewilderment in the face of political realities. Who is responsible? Haven't the farcical trials which have deliberately distracted attention from the reality of terrorism created that confusion which results in his extremism? Her son is the child of parents who have lived

198

through the *contestazione* and its aftermath, the *riflusso*.
He is the victim of the political situation in Italy, whereby
it has become virtually impossible to organise an effective
opposition in the government. The Italian political scene
gives the impression to foreigners of being in a constant
state of flux, since there is a change of government
apparently every few months; the reality is very different.
Because of the inexhaustible ability of political parties to
form advantageous alliances, Italy has been governed
since the Second World War by a series of coalition
governments. The two-party system which is so familiar
in Britain and America does not exist in Italy. The
opposition is clearly between the Communist Party, on
the one hand, and the right-wing Christian Democrat
Party, on the other. But, because of their skill in forming
alliances with the smaller parties, the Christian Democrats
have remained in effective control for forty years. Craxi's
brilliant manipulation of the 'Pentapartito' when he
brought his own (Socialist) party to power in 1985 is the
perfect example of how the alliance of the Christian
Democrat and Socialist parties with the three major
*partitini* (little parties) – the Republicans, the Social
Democrats and the Liberals – has managed to keep the
Communists from power. And it illustrates how a few
*cavalli di razza* (horses with a pedigree, i.e. leading power-
brokers) such as Andreotti, Spadolini and (Fo's own *bête
noire*) Fanfani have succeeded in dominating the Italian
political scene for decades. An attempt to curb the power
of this political Mafia was mounted via terrorism – the last
resort of those disillusioned with the failure of the radical
movements of the sixties – and the son in *The Mother* is
the victim of this system.

The most disturbing feature of this monologue is
therefore the way in which Rame can point an accusing

finger at the audience for their own complicity in the tragedy which has overtaken this woman. The most effective moment in the piece comes when the mother, after expounding the significance of the events of the sixties and having gained the audience's nodding complicity, announces that she is going to project a film in which, perhaps, some of the audience will see themselves involved in political action which they have since renounced. It is a clever *coup de théâtre*, reminding the audience of their own political history and their rejection of its implications. The jumps in time take us back to the sixties and – more precisely, in a sequence extended in detail – to the time when the woman's son brought home a friend who was sheltering from the police. The mother narrates this episode to illustrate her own betrayal not only of her son, but also of the ideals she once held and which she clearly had passed on to him. The self-accusation is pointed simultaneously at the audience. With the ninth section we again jump in time – to the mother's visit to the Sardinian prison where her son is incarcerated. She relates the indignities heaped on the women who have gone there to visit their sons. The last section translates the insupportable reality of this situation into a nightmare as the mother imagines that she is the sole custodian of her son and in a court trial loses him, only to find a child on the floor, covered in bruises and blood. At first she takes this child to be a friend's son who is being destroyed as a drug addict, but then she recognises him as her own son. As she holds him up to the judge she realises that he is dead. And the question with which this account confronts the audience is, who is responsible? It is easy, argues Rame, to blame the restrictive forces of the state, but this monologue asks more searching and disturbing questions which relate to the recent political history of Italy and to the responsibility of those who have lived through the dramatic confrontations of the sixties and the extremes of political violence and inactivity which have followed. This work is much more than a condemnation of the judiciary or the police force (though that is part of its aim): it is a challenge to its audience to face political realities and come to terms with the past.

It is not insignificant that *The Open Couple* hit considerable censorship difficulties. Fo and Rame were informed that the 'entertainment' was unsuitable for children under eighteen. The objections of the censor were to the one-act comedy and to the monologue *The Rape*. Intriguingly, no criticism was made of the far-more challenging political piece, *The Mother*. But this is not surprising. The challenge in *The Mother* is not to the *status quo* in Italy, but to the demoralised Left. There is nothing in this monologue that would disturb the consciences of the Right, convinced of the infamy of revolutionary terrorism. But the fact that minors might witness the comedy and the account of the rape was another matter. Rame's response was straightforward and sensible: she pointed out in a letter dated 22 December 1983 to the minister responsible that it was absurd to ban an unemotive, non-visual description of an assault of this nature when every night television offered endless graphic descriptions of rape and violence with no end other than to titillate the viewer. Anyone who has witnessed the trash which floods through the limitless channels of Italian television would appreciate her point instantly – and that of all those who have fought assiduously to prevent the (inevitable) advent of cable and satellite broadcasting in Britain. The objections to *The Open Couple* itself are more interesting. That the censor should find this play capable of corrupting the minds of younger theatre-goers is, in the last analysis, an acknowledgement of the political force of that underestimated dramatic genre, the comedy of manners.

# Envoi

Uno spettacolo non è mai come un altro. Le battute che funzionano una volta non funzionano, forse, dieci giorni dopo. Io devo controllare ogni sera gli applausi coll'uso del registratore, scrivendo subito le trovate nuove che suscitano risate e applausi. Per esempio questo spettacolo è andato male a Roma e anche a Bologna. Adesso, qui a Milano si gode di un successo clamoroso, e sai perchè? Perchè il testo originale – quello appena stampato – era dal tutto diverso. La prima scena è stata complettamente riscritta da Dario e tante altre cose sono state aggiunte o tagliate. Il lavoro sul testo, quindi, non è mai finito.

[One show is never the same as another. The jokes that work one evening don't work, let's say, ten days later. I have to check the applause every night by using a cassette recorder and making a note straightaway of the new gags which make the audience laugh or applaud. This show, for instance, went down very badly in

Bologna and Rome. And do you know why? Because
the original text – the one that's just been published –
was completely different. The first scene has been
completely rewritten by Dario and lots of other things
have been either added or cut. The work on the text,
therefore, is never over.]

(Franca Rame, interview with the author, Milan, 19
Feb 1987)

These were the comments of Franca Rame in Milan
immediately after a performance there of *Il ratto della
Francesca* (*The Abduction of Francesca*), a play first
produced in Trieste in December 1986. It is a very familiar
Fo–Rame concoction: another play about a kidnapping,
this time of a woman, a wealthy banker; a very spirited
pot-pourri involving the disguising of Francesca's captors
as leading members of the government, mistaken identity,
priests who turn out to be the organisers of the kidnapping,
double-crossing and a double (alternative) ending. As a
satire on the wealthy Italian *alta borghesia* performed in
the Teatro Ciak (a converted cinema on the outskirts of
Milan) to a predominantly well-to-do middle-class (and
middle-aged) audience, it represents the Fos' current
theatrical situation: the presentation of topical, highly
entertaining political satire to a mixed, but largely left-of-
centre, audience.

Dining with Franca Rame after the performance, I
found it difficult to believe that this elegant and beautiful
woman, who was capable of both talking and listening
with great enthusiasm, had just finished playing the lead
in a long and taxing show. She gave no sign of her age
(she was born in 1930), still less of the effect of the
astounding news she had imparted to a stunned Italian

nation just a fortnight before: that the time had come to make a break with Dario Fo. On a popular Sunday chat show, *Domenica in*, interviewed by a pushy and insensitive Raffaela Carrà, who insisted on probing into Dario Fo's reputation as a philanderer, Franca Rame came out with this revelation. Driving the knife further in the wound, Carrà asked if Fo knew of this, to receive the reply that he did not – that the decision was hers, made on the spur of the moment.

Accusations of exploitation were soon made: that Rame – woman of the theatre as she is – had taken advantage of the situation to make a highly dramatic gesture. It certainly came as a surprise to Fo, then in Holland working on a production of *The Barber of Seville* (*o tempora! o mores!*) and to their son Jacopo, who, when interviewed by the magazine *L'espresso*, said that, though things had clearly been far from well between his parents for some time, the announcement of the separation on television had been a great shock to him. He made it very clear, however, that his mother was in no way exploiting the situation: she was incapable of faking. Why should you be so surprised, he asked the interviewer, that she told the truth? After all, she was under great pressure and in a vulnerable, exposed position on television both as a woman and as an actress.

Besides, he added, anyone who had been following his parents' career and the plays they had been performing together over the last few years could scarcely have been unduly surprised at the announcement. Since *Parliamo di donne* – and more recently with the creation of the monologues – Rame has emerged very firmly as an actress in her own right: not, of course, entirely independent of Fo, but with a new, powerful personality born of the struggles – those of the women's movement particularly –

in the seventies and with a more vitally creative role in the partnership. *The Open Couple* we must now read as a far more personal document. Fo, since the announcement of the separation, has made it clear that this play was far too close to home for him ever to have played the part of the husband. And the more recent drama *Parti femminili* (1986) – literally *Female Parts*, in some respects a nod in the direction of the British version of *Tutta casa, letto e chiesa* – is clearly not without autobiographical significance. It is a play about a woman separated from her husband who, in attempting to commit suicide, is constantly interrupted by (misrouted) phone calls from women more desperate than herself.

It says something about the significance of Fo and Rame in Italy that the announcement of the separation should have proved so newsworthy. Pinter's betrayal of Vivian Merchant and subsequent marriage to Lady Antonia Fraser was not a matter of much concern to the British general public. But Fo and Rame are an institution. They have personified popular Italian culture for over thirty years, both as performers and as man and wife. In some respects their separation represents a more significant split within Italian society. Divorce is on the increase – the inevitable consequence of the failure of the open couple. It was profoundly disturbing for the millions of viewers who saw that edition of *Domenica in* – a programme which goes out at peak family viewing-time on Sunday afternoon and is designed to bolster conservative middle-class values – to learn of the failure of what is perhaps Italy's most celebrated marriage. In that respect Rame (perhaps subconsciously) knew what she was doing in allowing this bomb to explode in the face of so many viewers.

Rame has, however, lost nothing of her commitment to theatre, as she revealed whilst we were dining, showing me the tapes that had been made of the previous performances and her sheets of paper with lists of the gags that had worked and of the excisions which would be necessary. She was just as precise in her notes – often far from kind – to the members of her company who had miscalculated gags (and shown a lack of professionalism) by relying too much on what had worked in previous performances. She emphasised that no two performances were ever the same and that it was necessary as a performer to have one's antennae acutely trained to the slightest response from the audience: never to expect laughs and never to destroy them.

These observations not only underlined the fact that Rame comes from a celebrated family of theatrical performers, but also reminded me of the approach of a very different – but no less professional – writer and actor of comedy: Noel Coward. The extraordinarily precise observation and codification of the relationship between dramatic material and audience response, while maintaining an easy and apparently improvisational style of performance, represents the most basic of theatrical paradoxes: that summed up so wittily by Coward when he said, of a television series in which he performed with Mary Martin, 'The show will be completely spontaneous, the kind of spontaneity I like best, the kind that comes after five weeks of rehearsal' (quoted in Dick Richards, *The Wit of Noel Coward*, 1962).

*Il ratto della Francesca* is the perfect example of the way Fo and Rame work. Though a highly diverting comedy with a zany (but logical) plot which unfolds with great brio, constantly surprising us with new twists, it has a strong political – and ultra-topical – satirical basis. Few works of Fo in recent years have given such a clear impression of his adoption of what is essentially a

207

*commedia dell'arte* approach to theatre. The plot is a scenario – constantly adapted during performance – which is capable of improvisation according to changing circumstances. This was clearly illustrated in the first performance I witnessed. When Franca Rame launched into a satiric monologue on the rich, comparing the stupidity of their Dobermann guard dogs to that of the Savoy family (and their monarchist supporters), a man jumped up at the back of the stalls railing against this unfair attack – on the Dobermann! It seemed a crazy episode straight out of a Fo play – *Archangels*, to be precise. In fact it was no such thing. Franca Rame assured me the man was no plant, but, as she had learned from his wife in the interval, someone whose dog had recently died and who was disturbed. The way Rame handled the situation was exemplary and gave rise to a whole string of fresh jokes in the performance the following night.

A further aspect of *commedia* was to be seen in the skilful use of masks. Throughout the play, the four members of the gang who have kidnapped Francesca put on masks to avoid being recognised. These were highly detailed and represented the leading right-wing political figures: Craxi, de Mita, Spadolini and Andreotti. The transformation of the kidnappers into these figures was a *coup de théâtre* which delighted the audience, and which was subsequently to take on the force of symbol as an allegory of the manipulation of wealth by these political criminals developed. The masks gave rise to an endless series of gags: as when Francesca, speaking of another political kidnapping, turned to one of the gang and said, 'You must know all about this!' – thereby addressing Andreotti. When the leader – masked as Reagan – finally turned up, the gang-member wearing the Spadolini mask, having made a critical mistake, rushed over to him to be stroked on the head and cuddled. The comedy of *La signora è da buttare*, or of the Mayakovsky dance drama in *The Worker*, was profoundly re-evoked.

Another aspect of the play's political satire is seen in the way the first act was reworked. Rame informed us after the second performance I attended that the whole of Act I had been rewritten – after the opening in Trieste – as a satire on the panic generated in Italy over AIDS. This may not seem to a British – still less to an American – audience a subject for comedy. It is difficult to imagine any other dramatist who would have his main character make her first entrance with a blindfolded stranger whom she has brought back as a lover only to subject him to a protracted blood test. Treated, as he says, like a calf before it is slaughtered, he demands with some justification to know whether or not she is body positive, whereupon she produces full medical confirmation to the contrary on a small plastic card which she states ought to become as obligatory as an identity card or, more appropriately perhaps, a driving licence. In a stand-up routine later she discussed the implications of AIDS with the audience, commenting, with marked irony, that Italian wives have welcomed the disease. All those excuses their husbands used to make to pop out for a clandestine, casual (and, in Italy, often homosexual) encounter have stopped. Talking so openly about these issues, challenging prejudice, combating ignorance and defusing panic are, however, contributions at least as valuable as government campaigns, which in Britain have served initially to generate terror.

It would be unwise to predict what will happen next in the career (or careers) of Fo and Rame. There is hope that, if a permanent separation does ensue, the theatrical relationship will not be destroyed. It cannot but be changed, however, as Chiara Valentini was quick to point out in her article in *Panorama* soon after news of the separation broke. At this stage it is Valentini who should be allowed the final word:

> Perhaps a separate – autonomous – existence is in store for this most anti-traditional of actresses, the leading figure in so many theatrical and political issues during the last few years. But there can be no doubt that Franca Rame has already realised her first piece of directing independent of Fo – in front of a television audience in the company of Raffaela Carrà.
>
> (*Panorama*, 15 Feb 1987)

# Bibliography

## Performed and published works

Works listed in chronological order of first performance. Details following title relate to publication. The following abbreviations are used for collected editions:

Commedie — *Le commedie di Dario Fo*, 6 vols (Turin: Einaudi, 1966, 1966, 1975, 1976, 1977, 1984)

Compagni senza censura — *Teatro politico di Dario Fo*: *compagni senza censura* (Milan: Mazzotta, 1970, 1973; 2nd edn 1977).

Teatro comico — *Teatro comico di Dario Fo* (Milan: Garzanti, 1962). Republished as Vol. vi of *Commedie*.

1952 *Poer nano*, by Dario and Jacopo Fo (Milan: Ottaviano, 1976).
1953 *Il dito nell'occhio*, in *Teatro d'oggi* (Milan), ii, no. 3 (1954).
1954 *I sani da legare*, in *Sipario* (Milan), 1955.
1958 *Ladri, manichini e donne nude*, in *Teatro comico*; *Commedie*, vol. 6.
1958 *Comica finale*, in *Teatro comico*; *Commedie*, vol. 6.
1959 *Il novecentonovantanovesimo dei mille*, in *Poer nano* (Milan: Ottaviano, 1976).
1959 *Gli arcangeli non giocano a flipper*, in *Commedie*, vol. 1.
1960 *Aveva due pistole con gli occhi bianchi e neri*, in *Commedie* vol, 1.
1961 *Chi ruba un piede è fortunato in amore*, in *Commedie*, vol. 1.
1963 *Isabella, tre caravelle e un cacciaballe*, in *Commedie*, vol. 2; *Compagni senza censura*, vol. 1.
1964 *Settimo: ruba un po' meno*, in *Commedie*, vol. 2.
1965 *La colpa è sempre del diavolo*, in *Commedie*, vol. 2.
1966 *Ci ragiono e canto* (Milan: Nuovo Canzoniere Italiano, 1966).
1967 *La signora è da buttare* (Turino: Einaudi, 1974)

211

# Dario Fo and Franca Rame

1968    *Grande pantomima con bandiere e pupazzi piccoli e medi*, in *Commedie*, vol. 3.

1969    *Ci ragiono e canto 2* (Verona: La Commune–Bertani, 1972). Also in *Commedie*, vol. 5.

1969    *Mistero buffo* (Milan: Nuova Scena, 1969; Verona: La Comune-Bertani, 1973). Also in *Compagni senza censura*, vol. 1; *Commedie*, vol. 5.

1969    *L'operaio cognosce tecento parole, il padrone mille*; *per questo lui è il padrone* (Milan: Nuova Scena, 1969). Also in *Compagni senza censura*, vol. 1; *Commedie*, vol. 3.

1969    *Legami pure che tanto io spacco tutto lo stesso* (Milan: Nuova Scena, 1969). Also in *Campagni senza censura*, vol. 1; *Commedie*, vol. 3.

1970    *Vorrei morire anche stasera se dovessi pensare che non è servito a niente* (Verona: La Comune–Bertani, 1970). Also in *Compagni senza censura*, vol. 2; *Commedie*, vol. 4.

1970    *Morte accidentale di un anarchico* (Verona: La Comune–Bertani, 1970; Turin: Einaudi, 1974). Also in *Campagni senza censura*, vol. 2.

1971    *Tutti uniti! tutti insieme! ma scusa, quello non è il padrone?* (Verona: La Comune–Bertani, 1971). Also in *Compagnie senza censura*, vol. 2; vol. 4.

1971    *Morte e resurrezione di un pupazzo* (Milan: La Comune–Sapere, 1971).

1972    *Fedayn* (Milan: La Comune–Sapere, 1972). Also in *Compagni senza censura*, vol. 2; *Commedie*, vol. 4.

1972    *Ordine, per Dio.OOO.OOO.OOO!* (Verona: La Comune–Bertani, 1972).

1972    *Pum, pum! Chi è? La polizia!* (Verona: La Comune-Bertani, 1972). Also in *Compagni senza censura*, vol. 1.

1973    *Ci ragiono e canto 3* (Verona: La Comune–Bertani, 1973).

1973    *Guerra di popolo in Cile* (Verona: La Comune–Bertani, 1974).

1974    *Ballate e canzoni* (Verona: La Comune–Bertani, 1974; Rome: Newton Compton, 1976).

1974    *Non si paga, non si paga!* (Milan: La Comune, 1974)

1975    *Il Fanfani rapito* (Verona: La Comune–Bertani, 1975).

1975    *La giullarata* (Verona: La Comune-Bertani, 1975).

1976    *La marjuana della mamma è la più bella* (Verona: La Comune-Bertani, 1976).

1977    *Tutta casa, letto e chiesa*, by Franca Rame and Dario Fo (Milan: La Comune, 1977; Verona: La Comune–Bertani, 1978).

1978    *La storia di un soldato* (Milan: Elekta, 1979).

1979    *La storia della tigre e altre storie* (Milan: Edizioni F. R. La Comune, 1980).

# Bibliography

1981 *Clacson, trombette e pernacchie* (Milan: Edizioni F. R. La Comune, 1981).
1981 *Tutta casa, letto e chiesa*, new (Milan: Edizioni F. R. La Comune, 1981).
1981 *L'opera dello sghignazzo* (Milan: Edizioni F. R. La Comune, 1981).
1982 *Il fabulazzo osceno* (Milano: Edizioni F. R. La Comune, 1982).
1983 *Coppia aperta – quasi spalancata* (Milan: Edizioni F. R. La Comune, 1984).
1984 *Quasi per caso una donna, Elisabetta*, in *Ridotto* (Rome), 1984.
1985 *Hellequin, Harlekin, Arlekin [Arlecchino]*, in *Alcatraz News* (Perugia), 1985.
1986 *Parti femminili* (Milan: Edizioni F. R. La Comune, 1986).
1986 *Il ratto della Francesca* (Milan: Edizioni F. R. La Comune, 1986).

## Unperformed and published works

1960 *Storia vera di Piero d'Angera che alla crociata non c'era* (Milan: Edizioni F. R. La Comune, 1981).

## Performed and unpublished works

1973 *Basta con i fascisti!*
1977 *Parliamo di donne*
1979 *La fine del mondo* (*Dio li fa e poi li accoppia*)

## English translations

*We Can't Pay? We Won't Pay!*, tr. Lino Pertile, adapted by Bill Colville and Robert Walker (London: Pluto Press, 1978). Revised as *Can't Pay? Won't Pay!* (Pluto Press, 1982).

*Accidental Death of an Anarchist*, tr. with an introduction by Suzanne Cowan, in *Theater*, 10, no. 2. (Spring 1979).

*Accidental Death of an Anarchist*, tr. Gillian Hanna, adapted by Gavin Richards (London: Pluto Press, 1980).

*'Ulrike Meinhof' and 'Tomorrow's News'*, tr. Tony Mitchell, in *Gambit*, 9, no. 36 (1980).

*Female Parts*: *One-Woman Plays*, tr. Margaret Kunzle, adapted by
   Olwen Wymark (London: Pluto Press, 1981).
*About Face*, tr. Dale McAdoo and Charles Mann, in *Theater*, 14, no. 3
   (Summer–Fall, 1983).
*Trumpets and Raspberries*, tr. and adapted by R. C. McAvoy and A.
   M. Giugni (London: Pluto Press, 1984).

## Critical studies in Italian

There are a large number of books on Fo. The following is a select list.

M. Cappa and R. Nepoti, *Dario Fo* (Rome: Gremese, 1982). This is a
   large, copiously illustrated volume covering all of Fo's work up to
   1982. Its format, with hundreds of production photographs and extracts
   from reviews presented chronologically, makes it useful even for non-
   Italian readers.
C. Valentini, *La storia di Dario Fo*, (Milan: Feltrinelli, 1977). This is
   the most exhaustive account to date of Fo's career. It is written by a
   journalist, not a dramatic or literary critic and does not attempt to
   analyse the plays.
L. Binni, '*Attento te . . . .*' *Teatro politico di Dario Fo* (Verona: Bertani,
   1975). This study is based on a series of interviews and lengthy extracts
   from Fo's work.
C. Meldolesi, *Su un comico in rivolta. Dario Fo*: *il bufalo, il bambino*
   (Roma: Bulzoni, 1978). An analysis of Fo's theatrical technique and
   significance as a political dramatist.

## Other material available in English

T. Mitchell, *Dario Fo*: *People's Court Jester* (London: Methuen, 1984).
   This is the only previous study of Fo in English – a short one, dealing
   with all his work in chronological order.
*Red Notes. Dario Fo and Franca Rame*. Workshops at Riverside Studios,
   London, April and May, 1983 (London, 1983). Includes useful
   interviews with Fo and Rame as well as texts of *Waking Up, I Don't
   Move, I Don't Scream, my Voice is Gone* (*Lo stupro*) and *The Mother*.
'Dialogue with an Audience' and 'Popular Culture', two pieces by Fo
   translated by Tony Mitchell, are available in *Theatre Quarterly*, IX,
   no. 35 (Autumn 1979), and *Theater*, 14, no. 3 (Summer–Fall 1983),
   respectively.

# Bibliography

Two useful articles are S. Cowan, 'The Throw-away Theatre of Dario
Fo', *Drama Review*, 19, no. 2 (June 1978); and J. Schechter, 'Dario
Fo's Obscene Fables'. *Theater*, 13, no. 1 (Winter 1982).
There is a chapter on Fo by Lino Pertile in the volume *Writers and
Society in Contemporary Italy*, ed. M. Caesar and P. Hainsworth
(Leamington Spa: Berg, 1984).

# Index

With the exception of *Mistero Buffo*, all plays discussed in detail in this study are listed here under their English title. The rest are given their original Italian title.

# Index

*Index*